D1426536

PATRICK POIVRE D'ARVOR

First Class

Legendary Train Journeys
Around the World

THE VENDOME PRESS

4

Contents

1 ı A steam engine in Kenya.
2 ı Simplon-Orient Express
passengers stretching their legs
on a Bulgarian station platform.
4 ı The Orient Express in Milan
Central Station, 1930.
6 ı A halt at a station in northern
Canada.

ALL ABOARD! ALL ABOARD!

Luxury gets a bad press nowadays. For many people luxury is synonymous with all that is pointless and superfluous, with shameless waste and money thrown away. In fact quite the opposite is true. Luxury can even be a philosophy of life. Neither enslavement nor addiction, it is a key to freedom.

Since the mid-twentieth century, air travel has become increasingly easy and affordable. Yet there are still—and as long as there are railways there always will be—travelers who prefer the freedom, comfort or exoticism of taking the train. To take the train is to take your time, to travel at a human pace, or almost. To watch the world outside the window, the landscapes unfolding and the stations springing to life; and to watch the world inside, exchanging glances and sometimes conversation with your fellow passengers. And, when the mood suits you, to look inside your-self, lulled into thought—or indeed slumber—by the leisure of time, the gentle swaying and the rhythmic

clickety-clack of the wheels.

Like planes, modern trains generally serve merely to transport passengers from point A to point B. Modern trains go fast, or in the case of the TGV very fast, sometimes going half as fast as a plane. They can go even faster, indeed, and if the engineers have anything to do with it they will. This is not cause for complaint, of course, but now and then we may be allowed to indulge in the luxury of nostalgia for the golden age of railway travel, in the days when trains had not yet lost some of their magic.

O give me your magical muffled rumbles
And the resonance of your birdsong,
Orient Express, Sud-Brenner-Bahn;
Give me the light, easy exhalations
Of tall, slender locomotives with their
Flowing motion, of express engines
Effortlessly pulling four yellow carriages with
gold lettering

Through the lonely mountains of Siberia,
And the rose-filled valleys of Bulgaria…

So wrote Valéry Larbaud in *Les Borborygmes* (The Rumblings) a century ago, in 1908—although in some ways he could have been writing yesterday; for how many of us feel with him that "I need these sounds and this motion in my poetry to express all that is inexpressible in my life, my childhood which sought to know nothing, only to hope eternally for things that were vague and indistinct."

Give me your great cacophony of noise, the
smoothness of your speed,
As you glide by night through the lights of Europe,
O luxury train!

In those days all writers and poets were in love with trains. Sometimes the attraction was even sensual, as man and machine merged into one. In the film version of Zola's *La Bête Humaine*, the camera dwelt lovingly on the well-oiled muscles of Jean Gabin, echoing the gleaming flanks of his engine. As train drivers became one with their locomotives, so passengers merged with the cosseted interiors of the carriages:

All these great grey carriages, tightly closed,
Gleaming silently in the autumn rain,
Their lettering faded, their endless rest.
Their abandoned nights, their pale windows…
O those darkened carriages, breathing in the night!
The fluttering of their blue-shaded lamps…
The train that passes by with a wail of pain…
I love those rain-washed trains as they slide
between the fields

Henry Bataille, *Le Beau Voyage*

A trip on a train is not a journey but a voyage; we do not drive, we navigate. It may sway and roll, but we feel safe in our own personal cocoon. And sometimes this, and no more, is what the luxury consists of: comfort, and being as far from the routine of everyday life as it is possible to be.

In the decades that preceded the golden age of railway travel there was a bronze age, the age of the railway pioneers, who crisscrossed plains and prairies, largely virgin land, with their tracks. In America the "Iron Horse" pushed ever further across the plains towards the mysterious Far West. And at the same time and on virtually every continent, men paid for this passion for leaping rivers, crossing mountain ranges and excavating tunnels with their sweat, and sometimes with their lives. It is to them that we owe this extraordinary network that links different peoples and destinies the world over. My thoughts have often turned to them while hurtling through the Gotthard Tunnel, the Simplon Tunnel, and now the Channel

Tunnel. It is thanks to the bold vision of the railway builders of those heroic times that later generations have been able to give free rein to their desire to dream, to escape.

Thanks to them, distant lands were opened up for all. Streamlined and razor-sharp, railways cut a path through steppe and taiga, snow-capped mountains and birch forests. They ploughed through jungles and deserts, speeding without pause through some of the most dust-dry regions on earth. Everything passes, they say; thanks to the railways and their golden age, however, everything passes much more quickly and elegantly.

The poetry of trains, like the poetry of railway stations, also has a long history, wreathed in the great clouds of steam that used to shroud the endless platforms, veiling from sight the weeping ladies and the grieving hearts. Though fond farewells on the footplate might have lost some of their charm with the passing of the age of steam, no one can deny that railway station adieus can still be imbued with a poignancy that is hard to find in the average airport departure lounge. Trains still move off slowly, first at walking pace and then—for those seeking that last wave or smile—at a brisk sprint. Then for long minutes the train lingers on in your frame of vision, creeping across the landscape until it finally dissolves into a dot on the horizon. And as it passes it leaves behind it, like all travelers, the imprint of its memory.

Railways have always offered inspiration for writers. This witer has undertaken many train journeys and written a lot on trains: an entire novel, a personal narrative, and a book on *Les Derniers Trains de Rêve*. Whenever I write on a train I feel inspired and serene, with just a lurking fear that the final destination will arrive too quickly, cutting me off in mid-flow. I have been fortunate enough to travel round the world by train twice for a reportage, and—even better—to take the train from Paris to Venice every weekend for a whole year, earning my

living in more prosaic fashion.

I have enchanted memories of my time working on the Orient Express. I loved the wood paneling, the exquisite décor and the tempting dishes that were whisked under my nose. The passengers would dress for dinner and the champagne flowed. When we slept, it was on uncomfortable board-like stretchers spread out along the corridors, in front of the illuminated boards that showed which passengers required our attentions.

My appetite whetted, I set out to go round the world by train, inspired by Albert Londres' observation in *La Chine en Folie* (1922): "When he traveled, it was like other people smoked opium or took cocaine. It was his vice. He was addicted to sleeping cars and steamers. And after years of aimless wandering across the face of the globe, he could vouch for the fact that neither a come-hither look from an intelligent…good-looking woman, nor the lure of a safe possessed for him the devilish charm of an ordinary small rectangular railway ticket."

My own railway travels have taken me on all the journeys in this book, starting with the legendary Orient Express, this time as a passenger. On its way to the mysterious orient, it passes through countries with equally fabled imperial pasts. The Austro-Hungarian empire has left its indelible mark on this railway that linked old Europe to the Ottoman empire, with Constantinople, formerly Byzantium and later Istanbul, as its ultimate destination. My own journey ended in Belgrade. During my subsequent wanderings through the country that was then still known as Yugoslavia, it seemed to me that traveling by train taught me a lot about the regions of Slovenia, Croatia, Serbia, Bosnia-Herzegovina, Kosovo, Macedonia and Montenegro. Every station had its own character, its own customs, its own dialect. Each conversation gave me useful tips about local customs, tastes and antagonisms. It seemed to me on that journey that I gained some insight into

the convulsions that would later tear the former Yugoslavia apart.

Train journeys through provincial France, by contrast, are considerably less eventful and more tranquil. Eighty "heritage" lines are still scattered throughout the country, with altogether some 700 kilometers of track. Most individual lines are under 10 kilometers long, but together they carry over three million passengers annually—equaling the number of visitors to Versailles. In Touraine and the Vivarais, enthusiasts can even learn how to drive a steam engine.

Among the most prestigious of French trains was the fabled Train Bleu, which for so long provided a luxury link between Paris and Nice, and on over the Italian border to Ventimiglia. Still there are some passengers who resist the speed of air travel, preferring a comfortable train journey, especially an overnight one, with all the charms of the old wagons-lits and the soothing rhythm of the bogies (plus the added attraction of avoiding all the searches and security measures, the lost baggage and the eternal delays).

Its namesake in the southern hemisphere, the Blue Train or Blou Trein, carries passengers from Cape Town to Pretoria amid the ultimate in modern luxury and comfort, even including full-size baths. In South Africa I also traveled on the Rovos Train, which runs about six times a month from Cape Town to Pretoria, sometimes with a leisurely excursion to the breathtaking Victoria Falls in Zimbabwe. The cabins are spacious, the dining fine and the service impeccable. The train makes two stops, first at an unlikely station, Matjiesfontein, now deserted, that has something of the feel of an American frontier settlement. All that survives there are a tiny automobile museum, where a few vehicles from the 1950s make you feel that the clock has stopped, and a hotel-bar that could be straight out of a western, complete with rocking chairs. The second stop is at the ghost town, or rather ghost mine, of Kimberley, which for centuries yielded diamonds beyond men's wildest dreams. What was then the world's largest open-cast diamond mine now holds a sky-blue lake deep in its bowels.

To the east, a jewel of a railway runs from Nairobi to Mombasa. This train too consists of refurbished vintage coaches, in a handsome ivory livery. Some of the coaches are over a century old, including the dining car with its busy and skilled crew of chefs and waiting staff. The lions of the Tsavo national park are now hard to spot, but when the line was under construction it was a different story: one bold lion dragged an official from a train in the middle of the night, and a pair of man-eaters terrorized a construction camp. When they were finally brought down, their skins were found to be peppered with burns and holes made by bullets and arrows. Not for nothing did the railway become known as the Lunatic Line.

The sumptuousness of life aboard the Lunatic Line is comparable only with the Palace on Wheels,

based on the opulent conveyances of the Indian maharajahs under the British Raj. Yet this is perhaps the most "artificial" of all the railways in this book: its route appears in no international timetable, and its itinerary is erratic, encompassing the beautiful sights of Delhi, Jaipur, Udaipur, Jaisalmer and Agra. So that its passengers can visit all these marvels, the train is nocturnal, and makes lengthy stops in crowded stations where sacred cows come and lick the compartment windows. The compartments are airy and spacious, with three or four per coach plus a shower, and an open bar car bringing up the rear of the train. As the coaches are not connected by vestibules, the train will stop in the middle of the countryside to allow passengers to make their way to the dining cars.

One of the finest teas in the world is served on the little Toy Train of Darjeeling, a reminder of British colonial derring-do and gentility that weaves a spectacular course through jungle and tea gardens in the highlands of India. Another train that runs through tea gardens is the much more recent Eastern and Oriental Express, less than two decades old but already a legend. From Singapore to Bangkok via Kuala Lumpur, it crosses three countries at the leisurely speed dictated by the jungle, a magnificent three-day journey with short visits to the island of Penang and the Bridge on the River Kwai.

There are other train journeys whose very names are an invitation to escape, such as the Trans-Siberian, the California Zephyr and the Canadian. Slowest of them all are the railways of the high Andes, climbing steep mountainsides with zigzags and switchbacks. As the train from Lima to Huancayo travels through the tunnel of La Galera, it reaches the highest point ever attained (until 2006) by passengers on a standard-gauge railway (the same height as Mont Blanc), surpassed only by the new Chinese railway through Tibet. As it crawls at a snail's pace past the abandoned railway station there, it is perfectly possible to jump on to the moving train, though only with care—not because of the speed, naturally, but because of the disorientating effect of the altitude. A first aider goes from carriage to carriage with an oxygen cylinder to minister to any suffering passengers. The Peruvians guard against altitude sickness by incessantly chewing coca leaves. Another railway in the high Andes gives access to Machu Picchu, on the way passing small children who amuse themselves by cutting through the vegetation, running faster than the train, to greet bewildered passengers afresh at every turn—hoping of course for a generous reward at journey's end.

After the formerly highest railway in the world comes one of the most northerly. From Toronto to Vancouver, via Jasper, the Canadian ploughs through ice and snow to link the eastern provinces to the Pacific across the world's second-largest country. Further south, the California Zephyr crosses the United States in barely three days, from Chicago to Denver, Salt Lake City and finally Oakland on the San Francisco Bay. In the land where air travel reigns supreme, passengers still choose the CZ for the comfort and the thrill of the journey, while for tourists its observation car offers magnificent panoramas of some of America's most dramatic scenery, including the Rocky Mountains.

Last but not least comes the railway that is perhaps the most legendary of all: the Trans-Siberian. Where other trains offer sybaritic opulence, the Trans-Siberian railway offers the romance of its name, and time—lots of it. Living in a train-shaped parallel world for eight days and seven nights presents its own challenges, as Peter Fleming recalled in *One's Company*, written in 1933:

Most men, though not the best men, are happiest when the question "What shall I do?" is supererogatory. ...That is why I like the Trans-Siberian Railway. You lie in your berth, justifiably inert. Past the window plains crawl and forests flicker. The sun shines weakly on an empty land. ...You have nothing to look at, but no reason to stop looking. You are living in a vacuum, and at last you have to invent some absurdly artificial necessity for getting up...And so the day passes. If you are wise you shun the regulation meal at three o'clock, which consists of five courses not easily to be identified...But as a matter of fact, what with the airless atmosphere and the lack of exercise, you don't feel hungry on the Trans-Siberian Railway. A pleasant lassitude, a sense almost of disembodiment, descends on you, and the food in the dining-car, which, though seldom really bad, is never appetizing and sometimes scarce, hardly attracts the vigorous criticism which it would on a shorter journey.

And so, as the train heads ever eastwards, you read and dream and drink tea from the samovar generously provided for all. At Irkutsk, five days out of Moscow, you face your first real decision: whether to go east to Vladivostok on the Trans-Siberian or the Trans-Manchurian, or to Beijing on the Trans-Mongolian, crossing a swathe of the Gobi Desert en route. Both destinations are tempting, and both have the merit of putting an end to the interminable journey. And as each train draws into its terminus and its passengers clamber out with their luggage, there will also be that poignant pang of regret, so familiar to all lovers of great railway journeys, that the journey is finally over.

Perhaps Blaise Cendrars should have the last word, from his beautiful prose poem of 1913 *Prosody of the Transsiberian and of Little Jeanne of France*, translated by John Dos Passos:

If I was a painter I'd splash a great deal of red,
a great deal of yellow on the end of this journey
Because we must all of us have been more or less
cracked

And an enormous delirium brought the blood

out on the drawn faces of my traveling companions.

As we drew nearer Mongolia

That roared like a burning building.

8 ı Saloon car on an American train, c. 1900.

11 ı Tables in a Pullman Orient Express dining car. In the 1980s, the Orient Express brought part of the Compagnie Internationale des Wagons-Lits rolling stock (officially classified a historic monument) back into service.

12 ı A train leaving the Gotthard Tunnel, 1880s. Opened in 1882, this tunnel provided a link from Belgium, the Netherlands and northern France through Switzerland to northern Italy.

17 ı The Simplon-Orient Express at the Turkish-Bulgarian border in the summer of 1950.

18 ı On the Lunatic Line between Nairobi and Mombasa, Kenya.

22 ı A phalanx of bellboys on the platform at Berlin awaits the arrival of a VIP visitor, 1900.

1881

THE TOY TRAIN OF DARJEELING

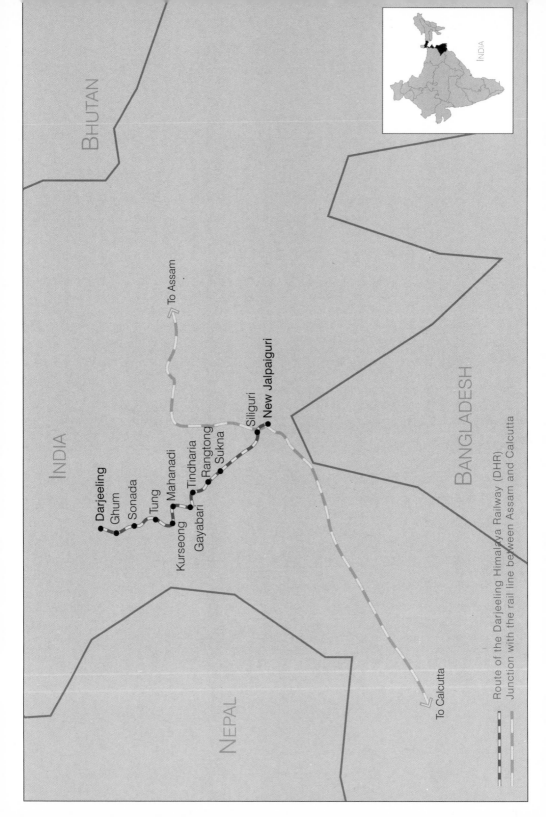

BHUTAN

INDIA

NEPAL

BANGLADESH

To Assam

Darjeeling
Ghum
Sonada
Tung
Mahanadi
Kurseong
Gayabari
Tindharia
Rangtong
Sukna
Siliguri
New Jalpaiguri

To Calcutta

Route of the Darjeeling Himalaya Railway (DHR)
Junction with the rail line between Assam and Calcutta

INDIA

U nder the Raj, it was the custom of British colonial society to escape in March every year to the cooler sanctuary of the Himalayan foothills, there to sit out the stifling summer heat of the plains. For almost six months of the year, eighty or more hill stations such as Mussoorie, Almora, Nainital and Ootacamund, perched at 2000m or higher, would suddenly spring to life, filled with young men in solar topees, memsahibs, children and servants, bringing with them an atmosphere as English as the climate allowed. Simla, summer home to the Viceroy, became the summer capital of the British Indian government, the contrast between life in the plains and the hill stations being mischievously summed up by William Thackeray as "duty and red tape; picnics and adultery." Darjeeling, "discovered" by a delegation of British East India Company officers in 1828, was valued for its breathtaking views of the Himalayas, its spectacular rhododendrons, its bracing climate and its refreshing drizzle—in some ways, indeed, one might almost think one was in England.

Thus it was that every summer trainload upon trainload of British administrators and officers, with their wives and families, would be deposited in the lower foothills of the Himalayas, to continue their journey by cart track. Carts, porters and ponies would be commandeered to haul memsahibs, children and servants up to the hill stations, with their panoplies of tin trunks and traveling boxes crammed with the essentials of life: Wedgwood dinner services, silver canteens, polo gear, picnic baskets, ballgowns and much, much more.

It was the extreme discomfort of this leg of the journey that led before long to the building of mountain railways. The idea of a railway to Darjeeling, the brain-child of Franklin Prestage, agent of the Eastern Bengal State Railway, was further encouraged by the develop-ment of tea gardens in the surrounding hills and the existence since 1870 of a railway line from Calcutta to the town of Siliguri, the terminus from which the great ascent into the hills began.

It was in 1878 that Prestage embarked on this daunting project, fraught with difficulties. Only a narrow-gauge line, 2ft or 610mm wide, could negotiate the narrow escarpments, for instance. This was an experiment that had already been tried with success on the Festiniog railway in Wales, constructed in 1836 to serve the slate mine of Blaenau Ffestiniog in the mountains of Snowdonia. Steam traction started in 1863 and the results were encouraging: so reliable and safe was the little narrow-gauge railway that in 1865 it started to carry passengers. But at Darjeeling the route was longer and the gradient steeper. Prestage and his team soon came up against apparently insuperable obstacles, and work ground to a halt. According to Darjeeling folklore it was his wife who hit upon the solution, so guaranteeing the railway's future. In the winter of 1878, the Prestages attended a ball at the Tindharia Planters' Club below Darjeeling. A great fire was roaring in the grate, guests were talking and

laughing and the orchestra played indefatigably, but Prestage was lost in thought: how could he push his railway up this unclimbable mountainside? Divining his thoughts, his wife gently drew him to the edge of the dance floor, before suddenly whirling him round and waltzing backwards to the middle of the floor, whispering into his ear as she did so, "If you can't go forwards, darling, go backwards!"

At Tung the train pauses to take on water, before climbing ever upwards to Sonada and on to Ghum, eternally shrouded in mist. The highest point of the journey coincides with its most daring feat of engineering, the Batasia Loop, and its most thrilling view, of the Kanchenjunga, the world's third-highest peak. Following this dizzying climb the train stops once more to take on water, before embarking on the precarious descent to its terminus at Darjeeling.

In 1999, the Toy Train and its vertiginous route, described by Unesco as an "outstanding example of bold, ingenious engineering solutions for the problem of establishing an effective rail link through a rugged, mountainous terrain," was inscribed as a World Heritage Site, an honor shared only by two other railways, the Nilgiri Mountain Railway in southern India and the Semmering in Austria.

Ticket for the Siliguri to Tindharia leg of the Darjeeling Himalayan Railway.

24 | B class locomotive B779 negotiating the Batasia Loop on 24 January 1994, against the spectacular backdrop of the Kanchenjunga. Soon it will arrive at Ghum, at 2258m the highest railway station in India. 779, built in 1889 by Sharp Stewart of Manchester, is one of the most venerable locomotives still plying this route.

At daybreak we could make out the silhouette of mountains through a light mist: these were the first foothills of the Himalayas, and the plains stretched unbroken to their feet. The train stopped at Siliguri Station, where we were invited to transfer to a little narrow-gauge railway, offering neither comfort nor reassurance, but apparently designed in such a way as to negotiate in resolute fashion the uncommonly steep inclines and bends that, in the space of nine hours, will take us up to Darjeeling at 7200 feet.

ÉMILE DELMAS, 1898

Zigzag on the Darjeeling rail line, circa 1895.

37 ı Locomotive 806 in the Darjeeling repair yard, February 2005. Built in 1928 by the North British Locomotive Company, this engine worked originally for the Raipur Forest Tramway in the state of Madhya Pradesh, before finally joining the Darjeeling Himalayan railway in August 1943.

38 ı Steaming through tea gardens, halfway between Siliguri and Sukna, where the railway track follows the road for some miles. This photo was taken from the roof of a local bus.

39 ı Children picking lumps of coal from the hot cinders on the railway line at Sukna station, February 2005. Once a familiar sight throughout India, this is now seen only on the Darjeeling Himalayan Railway.

40-41 ı From its inauguration to the year 2000, the Darjeeling Himalayan Railway was served exclusively by steam locomotives. Since 2005 the railway has used one oil-fired steam locomotive B class 787.

42 ı Just after Sukna Station and at the beginning of the climb, a train puffs through jungle still roamed by wild elephant. This a specially chartered day trip to adopted for a restricted service, and there are now four NDM$_6$ class diesels used on the line. A Walford diesel locomotive was tried in 1942, but the experiment was not conclusive and steam engines remained the most dependable method of scaling the gradients involved. In 2000, two diesel engines were nevertheless

The line follows the cart track, first of all through twelve miles of the unhealthy plains of Terai; then, rising ever more steeply, through a charming landscape of woods and forests, with admirable views to the far distance. Here the little train winds past magnificent trees dotted about on slopes swathed in luxuriant vegetation.

HUGUES KRAFFT, 1885

Agony Point: once there the passengers will disembark for the true purpose of their journey, a picnic inside the famous loop, before returning to Siliguri.

43 ǀ One of the most intriguing features of the line is the way the track runs right through the heart of villages en route, so the train chugs down main streets and

through bazaars, passing so close to stalls and shop-fronts that passengers can reach out and touch them.

44 ǀ The Chunbhati Loop in the late nineteenth century. On the ascent from Siliguri to Darjeeling at this period, the Chunbhati Loop was the third loop to be negotiated by the train. Since that

time the first two loops have been swept away by monsoon rains, leaving this as the first loop.

45 ǀ A nineteenth-century photograph of the catch siding at Bore Ghat, designed to bring runaway trains to rest. Local wags dubbed it the "Duke's Nose."

46 ǀ Agony Point, c.1890. The tightest loop on the line,

encountered just after Tindharia Station, Agony Point owes its name to the agonies endured here by those of a delicate disposition.

47 ǀ Agony Point as featured on the cover of a tourist brochure published c.1917.

48 ǀ A photochrome view of the Darjeeling region in the 1890s, set

As I write, this is what I see before me: in the foreground, along the ridge that we have just reached, the little villas of Darjeeling, white spots against the dark forests and the last outpost of civilization, the brink of the abyss where the wilds of Asia begin, that vast unknown land peopled by men with yellow skins. Then a great void of darkness, a vast amphitheatre filled with night and crossed by formless scraps of cloud. Five rays, thin and hazy, pierce the blackness, shot from a dazzling bulk crouched over the dark shoulder of the mountain behind us. No ocean, no desert on earth can rival the dizzying sense of emptiness aroused by these five straight lines catapulted across this valley, fifteen leagues broad and closed at the far end by a wall eight thousand meters high.

ANDRÉ CHEVRILLON, 1891

49 | In this verascope photograph of the entrance to the village of Kurseong, taken by Lafarelle on 4 November 1910, the railway tracks are clearly visible. After Kurseong, a picturesque cluster of shops and dwellings clinging to the mountainside, the snowy heights of Kanchenjunga can be seen looming in the distance.

50 | A photochrome of the environs of Darjeeling in c.1895. After the stifling heat of the plains, the British were enchanted by the snow-capped peaks, cool pine-scented air and refreshing landscape of lush green tea gardens to be found here, with the delightful addition on cloudy days of a touch of drizzle, so irresistibly reminiscent of home.

51 | Ghum Station, February 2005. However stifling the heat at Siliguri, passengers are likely to arrive at Ghum, the highest point on the line, to find it shrouded in mist. From mid-June to mid-September it is also quite likely to be raining.

A halt at Sonada Station, c. 1935.

At Siliguri we change carriages. The first foothills are now only twenty miles away, and the approach of a new world is palpable. Now, beside the tiny Bengalis, we begin to see short, stocky mountain dwellers with square faces and mongoloid features, yellow complexions and slanting eyes. They wear felt boots, three-bladed daggers stuck in their belts, and dark wool coats that contrast sharply with the brightly coloured robes of the Hindu women. This is the meeting point of two races, the frontier between two continents of humanity, for the Tatars, whose territory starts with the Himalayan foothills, cover Central Asia and China as far as they icy wastes of the Arctic Circle.

What an astonishing assortment of humanity is to be found in this little station in the middle of nowhere! A dozen British planters and officers and two or three Swedish and German tourists amid a sea of Hindus, Lepchas and Bhutanese. European jackets, white Bengali "skirts," the red dresses of the Lepcha women, almost Siberian in their features, jewels and clothes, and Tibetan greatcoats all squeeze together into open carriages looking rather like sleighs. The little locomotive whistles and we are off, heading for the great blue wall at the end of the plains

ANDRÉ CHEVRILLON, 1891

34

Darjeeling is one of the few places in India from which you can see (Mount Everest), to the extent that the prince of Himalayan peaks (at 8848m / 29,029ft) has been pressed into service as part of a highly successful tourist attraction: sunrise at Tiger Hill. Tiger Hill is a few kilometers outside Darjeeling: to see the sunrise you have to be at the top by five o'clock in the morning, which means leaving at four, as it takes a good half an hour by car followed by a steep half-hour scramble (the slothful do this on mule back, while those of stiffer mettle—myself included, obviously—climb up on foot, wrapped in a blanket, as at that time in the morning and at that altitude the cold is positively glacial).

Once at the top, everyone stamps their feet and blows on their fingers to warm up while waiting for "it" to appear. And it's well worth the wait, it has to be said. The spectacle of the snowy peaks gradually turning shades of pink, mauve, orange and brilliant red, before suddenly erupting in a conflagration at the precise moment when the scarlet globe pierces the horizon, is quite extraordinary. But to each his due: Everest still enjoys a lively reputation for legend and mystery, despite having twice been conquered, by British and Swiss climbers. But in my humble opinion the king of the Himalayas … is Mount Kanchenjunga. Everest, lofty and distant, only ever reveals its very tip, submerged by clouds … Kanchenjunga, on the other hand, unfolds itself in all its splendor before the dazzled gaze of mere mortals. In Darjeeling you never tire of looking at it.

CLAUDINE CANETTI, 1961

The
DARJEELING 
MOUNTAIN RAILWAY

1883

THE ORIENT EXPRESS

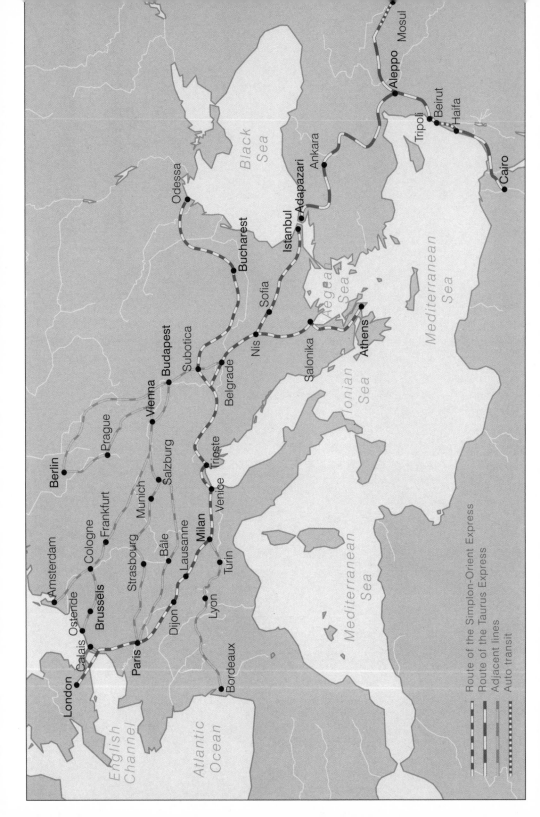

London
Calais
Ostende
Brussels
Amsterdam
Cologne
Frankfurt
Prague
Berlin
Paris
Dijon
Strasbourg
Bâle
Munich
Salzburg
Lausanne
Vienna
Budapest
Lyon
Milan
Turin
Venice
Trieste
Subotica
Belgrade
Bordeaux
Nis
Sofia
Bucharest
Odessa
Salonika
Athens
Istanbul
Adapazari
Ankara
Aleppo
Mosul
Tripoli
Beirut
Haïfa
Cairo

English
Channel

Atlantic
Ocean

Black
Sea

Aegean
Sea

Ionian
Sea

Mediterranean
Sea

Mediterranean
Sea

Route of the Simplon-Orient Express
Route of the Taurus Express
Adjacent lines
Auto transit

It was the painful ordeal of early railway travel that was responsible for ushering in the age of luxury trains. Honoré Daumier documented this prehistory of the railways in caricatures featuring morose-looking passengers being bounced, jolted and shaken mercilessly on hard wooden benches, usually squashed between a man smoking a foul-smelling pipe and a woman unpacking equally noisome victuals. Smuts from the engine and the odor of tightly packed humanity added a certain *je ne sais quoi* of exquisite discomfort. In the 1860s, train travel was scarcely more pleasant then the notoriously unappealing stagecoach. Railway journeys in Europe seemed interminable; in the United States they were ten times longer, and the tortures of the wretched train traveler were all the more insufferable. George Mortimer Pullman, a frequent traveler on the American railways, was a connoisseur of the hardships involved, complaining of the endless nights endured while perched on unyielding benches, shaken to within an inch of his life, shivering with cold, and peering through the gloom of the flickering candlelight.

In 1863 he decided to do something about it, setting up a modest workshop to build a new type of railway carriage, dubbed the Pioneer, in which passengers could lie down and rest on overnight journeys. He could not claim to have invented the sleeping car, as Cornelius Vanderbilt, king of the American railroad, had already commissioned such a novelty from the Webster Wagner coach-building works. In truth, Vanderbilt's sleeping cars were merely ordinary carriages with the seats replaced by proper beds. In a stroke of genius Pullman went a stage further, devising the first couchettes. In carriages laid out on either side of a central corridor, fold-away beds were pulled down at night to form the upper berths, while the seats were pulled out to form the lower berths; finally, curtains were pulled across to afford privacy to the gentleman or lady sleepers. The idea was both ingenious and highly profitable, as the carriages could carry as many passengers at night as they did during the day. And then came an invaluable public relations coup: following the assassination of President Lincoln in 1865, his widow, who had heard tell of these comfortable, luxurious railway carriages, asked for one to transport her husband's body from Washington to Kentucky. On the journey out, the carriage was saluted as it passed by grieving citizens; on the way back, it was besieged by visitors eager to see this remarkable carriage. Pullman's new career was launched.

At about this time there arrived in New York a young Belgian engineer and his mentor. The young man, Georges

Nagelmackers, was not traveling for pleasure, but rather—at his father's insistence—in order to wean him from an unsuitable affair of the heart. For ten months the young man rode the railroad from east to west and back again, experimenting with all forms of rail travel, and especially with the famous Pullman sleeping cars. In comparison with rail travel in Europe at the time, he found the level of comfort staggering. If he had one small criticism it was the flimsiness of the curtains, which—liable as they were to blow open in a draught—would certainly offend the morals of respectable European lady passengers.

Nagelmackers gave the matter a good deal of thought, and on his return to Belgium published a *Project for the Installation of Sleeping Cars on Continental Railways.* Though it did not perhaps make gripping reading, it nonetheless contained ideas of astonishing novelty. Pullman had developed the sleeping car-as-dormitory. Nagelmackers' invention was the sleeping compartment, with a door opening on to a corridor running along one side of the carriage: a device fit to save any lady's modesty. The secret of Nagelmackers' success, however, lay in his vision and determination, his independence from railway operators, and his ability to win the support of Leopold II, King of the Belgians. At this time European railways were steeped in

Poster by Choubrac for a musical comedy of 1896 entitled *Orient Express.*

Ancien ÉLYSÉE MONTMARTRE
TRIANON Concert
80
Bard ROCHECHOUART
Ancien ÉLYSÉE MONTMARTRE
COMPAGNIE INTERNATIONALE DES WAGONS LITS
ORIENT EXPRESS
VOYAGE EN 2 TABLEAUX de Mr. Oscar SACHS MUSIQUE de Mr. Henri NEUZILLET
DÉPART tous les soirs à 10 heures ½

and operated by Mann's Railway Sleeping Carriage Company throughout Europe. It was time to move up a gear. Night-time comfort was now complemented by day-time luxury, with the addition of the first *voiture-salon*, or saloon car, on the Nice-Menton route. In 1882, the first restaurant car was inaugurated between Marseille and Nice. The die was now cast: discerning travelers would tolerate nothing less than trains running on direct routes and equipped not only with sleeping cars but also with saloon cars, restaurant cars, and all other modern comforts. The next step was obvious: why not run a train composed

Sleeping arrangements in first class accommodation before the introduction of sleeping cars.

nationalism and hedged about with protectionism. In these circumstances, it may be imagined just how warm a welcome a Nagelmackers' sleeping car—this foreign rolling stock that could cross national frontiers at will—would receive in many quarters.

Nevertheless, with the support of King Leopold, Nagelmackers managed to secure the success in 1873 of the Paris-Vienna line, one of the most important and well-traveled routes in Europe. Other contracts followed, with all the companies involved undertaking to include at least one of Nagelmackers' sleeping cars on each of the specified trains. The problem lay in the finances: the sleeping car supplement paid by passengers was barely profitable, and certainly did not yield enough to encourage investors. To add to Nagelmackers' problems, Pullman had recently arrived in Europe, and was already making a name for himself in Britain and Italy. But success did finally come, the impetus being provided by passengers who, having tasted the comfort of travel by sleeping car, would settle for nothing less. Even the diplomatic difficulties seemed gradually to fade away.

On 4 December 1876, Nagelmackers founded the Brussels-based Compagnie Internationale des Wagons-Lits, taking over the 53 sleeping cars and 22 contracts owned entirely of these luxury carriages, in which passengers could live in comfort, as though in a hotel on rails? And why not a train that for the first time would run right across Europe, with no changes and no borders, as far as the Orient? Nagelmackers was now in the business of selling not only comfort but also dreams: hence the birth of the magnificent Orient Express, and of all the luxury trains that would follow in its wake.

The complications of setting up the Orient Express were considerable: each border crossing had to be negotiated with every nation and railway company concerned, with talks sometimes dragging on for months before agreement could be found. But on 4 October 1883, the Orient Express was ready for its maiden voyage, from Paris to Constantinople. It wasn't really an express, nor did it really go to the Orient (the through line was not completed until 1889), but the prominent figures who were invited as guests on that first journey returned to Paris dazzled by the experience. The journey was not considered to be without its perils, and just to be on the safe side, the gentlemen on board were earnestly exhorted to bring a pistol with them.

And so the glamour and drama of the Orient Express were born. The glamour of mahogany paneling, sofas upholstered in peacock-blue velvet, armchairs embossed in gold, glasses of finest crystal, and *sole meunière* served on silver dishes, while the engine whistled and wolves howled in the distant darkness. There was the drama of possible murderous attacks (always a risk in the Balkans), a cholera epidemic with all passengers quarantined, snow-drifts (in 1929 the train was cut off for a week 80km/50 miles outside Constantinople,) princes and schemers, ministers and spies, criminals and thunderbolts. Not to mention the lunatic King Ferdinand of Bulgaria, who on one occasion signaled the train to stop, leapt onto the engine, seized the controls and—deaf to the driver's entreaties—shot off at full steam. Then equally suddenly he brought the train to a shuddering, squealing halt. All he wanted to do, he explained, was test the brakes. Letters of complaint flooded into Nagelmackers' office, but the next service was still fully booked.

Aided by commercial success and political support, the Orient Express branched out in new directions, extending the network and giving birth to numerous offspring. In 1906, following the opening of the Simplon Tunnel, the Simplon Express was founded, becoming the Simplon-Orient Express in 1919. Combining the exoticism of the

Orient with honeymoon romance, the train now went to Turkey via Venice. From 1924, the Swiss-Arlberg-Orient Express served major stations in Switzerland and Austria, with carriages going on to Budapest, Bucharest, and Athens. In 1930, finally, with the creation of the Taurus Express, the Orient Express at last had a connection across the Bosphorus. The network had reached its apogee, stretching to Cairo, Tehran and Baghdad, and to Bombay by connecting P&O steamer from Marseille. Nagelmackers' dream had surpassed his wildest expectations.

On 20 May 1977, the Direct-Orient Express pulled out of the Gare de Lyon, heading for Istanbul. To the casual observer, the presence in its rake of one authentic sleeping car was the only indication that this was the last voyage of the Orient Express.

52 I Victoria Station, London, in the 1940s, the departure point for English passengers wanting to transfer to the Orient Express on the Continent.

65 I Gare de l'Est, Paris, c.1890. It was from this station, then known as the Gare de Strasbourg, that the Orient Express set off on its maiden voyage on 4 October 1883. Built between 1847 and 1852, the structure was designed by the architect Léonce Reynaud. Inset: An Orient Express luggage label.

66 I Orient Express locomotive, 1883.

67 I Pass authorizing a company employee to travel on the Orient Express: "no supplement payable."

68 I Menu for 17 April 1884. Six months after its launch, the Orient Express was still known officially as the "Train d'Orient."

69 I A restaurant car with its roof decorated in the Italian style characteristic of the years 1900–05. The most famous Orient Express restaurant car was no. 2419, built in 1913. On 15 October 1918, on the orders of the French Minister for War, it was refitted as an office and sent to join the train of Maréchal Foch at Rethondes in the Oise department. It was in this carriage that the Armistice was signed on 11 November. At Hitler's insistence, the altogether more painful armistice of 22 June 1940 was also signed there.

70 I The Budapest office of the Compagnie Internationale des

Hitherto, if one had a fortnight or so free and felt like a change of scene, one might have headed for the forest of Fontainebleau, or for some seaside town not too far from the Channel. Now one goes to Constantinople; as I have just done with some forty very agreeable fellow passengers. Having left the Gare de l'Est at seven-thirty in the evening on 4 October, we returned at six o'clock on the 16th, after spending a day in Romania and four and a half days in Constantinople.

For this marvel we have the Compagnie Internationale des Wagons-Lits to thank.

GEORGES BOYER, 1883

Wagons-Lits in 1914. Behind the imposing mahogany counter are ranged the clerks and ticket cabinets.

71 | Information leaflet published for passengers by the Compagnie Internationale des Wagons-Lits, 1900.

72-73 | The Orient Express in Bucharest Station, c.1905.

74 | A photochrome image of Tophane Square, Constantinople, c.1895.

75 | The drawing room of the Pera Palace Hotel in Constantinople, built in 1894 by the Compagnie Internationale des Wagons-Lits for passengers on the Orient Express. In the heat of summer, the hotel offered accommodation in its sister establishment, the Bosphorous Summer Palace Hotel at Therapia, on the shores of the Bosphorus.

76 | Left: a two-berth compartment in day-time formation, in one of the metal carriages built in Leeds in 1922. The marquetry is to a design by Morison. Right: Watercolour sketch by A. Toussaint for a poster advertising the times of Simplon Express trains between London and Venice.

77 | The Simplon-Orient Express at Isella Station, just after emerging from the Simplon Tunnel, in 1913. Linking Brig in Switzerland and Isella in Italy, the tunnel was opened in 1906. Three teams of miners, each 1500 strong, worked on the project in relays for eight years, encountering innumerable

So where are we? I have only the vaguest idea: somewhere between Pest and Temeswar. The train stops, and we are entertained by gypsy musicians. Actually these brilliant players are gypsies only in name. ...Bohemians or not, they've got the devil in them and they play with terrific panache. ...The engine whistles: music farewell! But no! The members of the band have leapt into the luggage van; soon they are in the dining car; there is a great commotion of tables and chairs being moved, and here are our young gypsies waltzing away furiously with the kind Viennese ladies. This little party only came to an end when we reached Szegedin.

EDMOND ABOUT, 1883

obstacles on the way, including pockets of toxic gas, rockfalls, underground rivers, and waterfalls of hot water that raised the temperature in the galleries to over 50 degrees Celsius.

78 | First class waiting room, Milan Central Station. With the inauguration of the Simplon Express, plans were put in hand for the rebuilding of the station in Milan which—standing as it did on the London-Venice-Constantinople line—was now one of the most prestigious in Europe. Although the project was launched in 1906, the splendid reconstruction work, by the architect Ulisse Stacchini, was not properly started until 1912.

79 | The Simplon-Orient Express at Milan Central Station, c.1940.

80 | Venice railway station in the 1880s. It was in 1861, under the Austrian occupation, that the first railway station was built in Venice, on the site of Palladio's church of Santa Lucia. When the Simplon Express later extended its route from Milan to Venice, it became the train for honeymooners. From that day to this, the station at Venice has remained the world's most romantic railway terminus.

81 | An antique Louis Vuitton trunk complete with Hotel Danieli sticker, memento of a luxurious trip to Venice.

82 | Trieste Harbour, c.1880. In its early days, the Simplon-Orient Express terminated at Venice. The Austrian authorities refused it access to Trieste, fearing that the luxury train would rival the ships

1921. A new stop in this station at Venice "that ends in nothing, in a great tank of shadow and silence"…. That day I was carrying on to Stambul, on a spanking new Simplon Express, intended by the Allies to dethrone the old Orient Express, first leg of Wilhelm II's *Baghdadbahn*. On terra firma, the trenches are filling in, and Venetian children are fishing in shell holes.

PAUL MORAND, 1983

of the powerful Austrian Lloyd company.

83 | The Gorges of the Danube, photochrome, c.1895. Until 1889 the Orient Express was not a through service. On their arrival at Giurgiu on the Danube, passengers transferred to a little steam packet for the voyage to Constantinople.

84 | The Simplon-Orient Express crossing a Greek viaduct in the 1920s.

85 | Left: Poster advertising the Simplon-Orient Express and the Taurus Express, by André Wilkin, 1930. Right: Toilet facilities in a sleeping car, 1902. Lavishly decorated with stained glass, the bathroom was situated between two cabins, which shared access to it. A bolt on the door leading to the other cabin ensured privacy for the occupier.

86 | Page from a brochure giving details of the entire Orient Express network, 1930-31. The map shown here plots the route of the Taurus Express line to Baghdad.

87 | The pyramids of Cairo, photochrome, c 1895. Cairo was the terminus of the southern branch of the Taurus Express.

The countryside, which had been flat and monotonous since the morning, became increasingly picturesque as we neared the Carpathians. Like the Danube, our route has its gates of Hell. Negotiating them is not always without its dangers: torrents take every opportunity to wash away the ballast; the green clay of the mountains crumbles or slides in great masses onto the railway track. Last week a train was derailed and there was loss of life, we are told. We spied a team of navvies working to avoid more accidents.

Our Saturday draws to its close amid magnificent and ever-changing scenery. Sadly night falls early in October; it crept up on us in the midst of the marvels of Herculesbad, the baths of Hercules, a resort that has been revived by the Romanians and decorated with infinite taste in the modern style … and so we cross into Romania in the dark.

EDMOND ABOUT, 1883

ORIENT-EXPRESS

Cᴵᴱ INᴸᴱ DES WAGONS-LITS
ET DES Gᴰˢ EXPRESS EUROPÉENS

...TERDAM-COLOGNE
...NNE - BUDAPEST
...BUCAREST

Paris — Gare de l'Est.

Compagnie Internationale des Wagons Lits
et des grands Express-Européens

CARTE PERSONNELLE

ORIENT-EXPRESS

1898

Monsieur Chevalier

Chef de la Comptabilité

est autorisé à voyager sans payer de supplément
dans le train dit : ORIENT-EXPRESS

Le Directeur Général:

N°.

N°. H5.

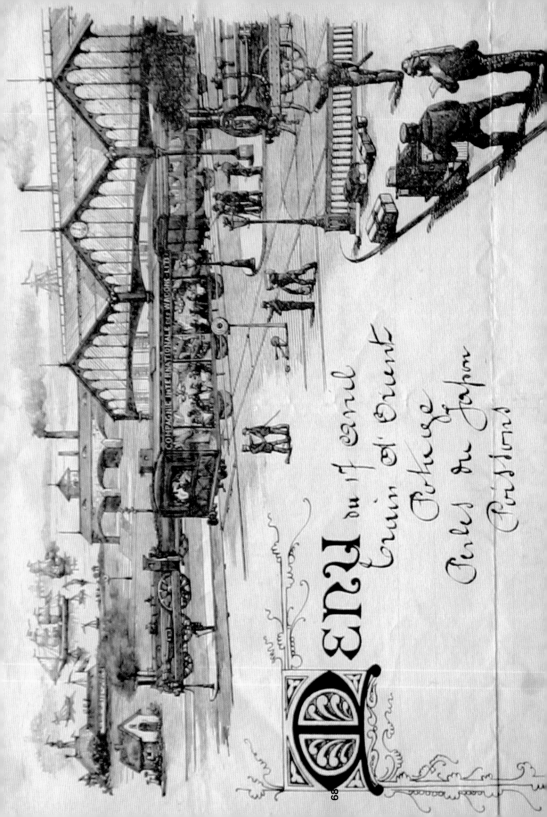

Paris

Train d'Orient

Portuge

Perles du Japon

Pensions

...-RRANÉE-EXPRESS, tri-hebdomadaire entre ... Paris (P.-L.-M.), Marseille, Nice, San-Remo et vice-versâ.
...-MÉDITERRANÉE-EXPRESS (Londres), Calais, Paris (Nord), Nice, San-Remo et vice-versâ, 4 fois
...-ROME-EXPRESS, bi-hebdomadaire entre les deux sens entre ST-PETERSBOURG-BERLIN-PARIS-VINTIMILLE
-PÉTERSBOURG-VIENNE-NICE-CANNES-EXPRESS } hebdomadaire dans les deux sens, quotidien
...XPRESS, Paris, Nice, Cannes et vice-versâ.
...LLE-BOMBAY-EXPRESS, ... hebdomadaire dans les deux sens.
DE LUXE direct bi-hebdomadaire voiture directe de et vers Porto et vice-versâ, 1 fois par semaine,
...SULAR-EXPRESS, Lisbonne à Pampilhosa, Madrid et vice-versâ, 2 fois par semaine.
...XPRESS, Train de luxe quotidien entre PARIS-BERLIN et vice-versâ. — OSTENDE-BERLIN et vice-versâ
...-T-EXPRESS, Paris, Vienne et vice-versâ.
...-VIENNE-EXPRESS } Londres, (Calais), Vienne et vice-versâ quotidien, Londres, Vienne, Trieste,
...-VIENNE-EXPRESS } Alexandre, hebdomad, Londres, Vienne, Constanza (Constantinople), hebdomad.
SUD (BRENNER)-EXPRESS Train de luxe quotidien entre BERLIN, LEIPZIG, MUNICH, MILAN et vice-versâ.

LISTE DES AGENCES DE LA COMPAGNIE DES WAGONS-LITS

Ce train transporte des colis messageries pour Vienne et au-delà. — Bureaux d'expéditions
40, Rue de l'Arcade, Paris.

ORIENT-EXPRESS

SERVICE QUOTIDIEN — Cie INTle DES WAGONS-LITS ET DES GRANDS EXPRESS EUROPÉENS

FÉVRIER 1900

MESSAGERIES DES GRANDS EXPRESS EUROPÉENS
40, rue de l'Arcade, Paris.

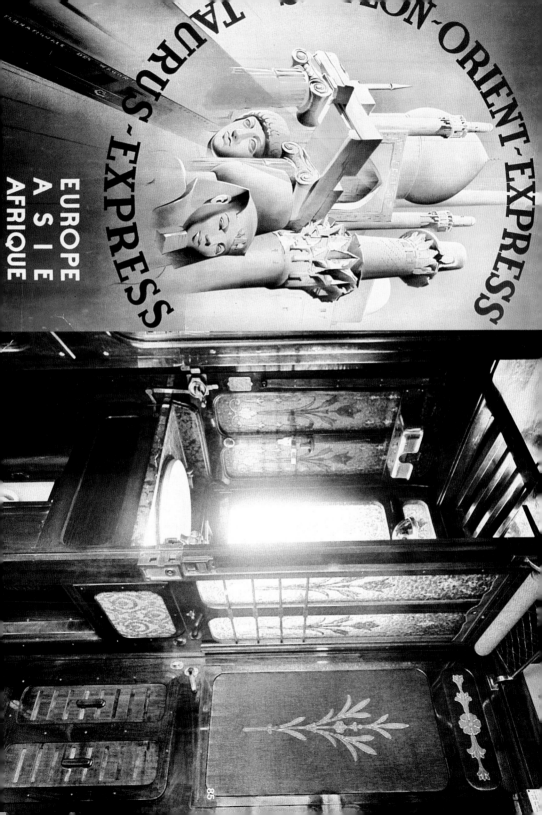

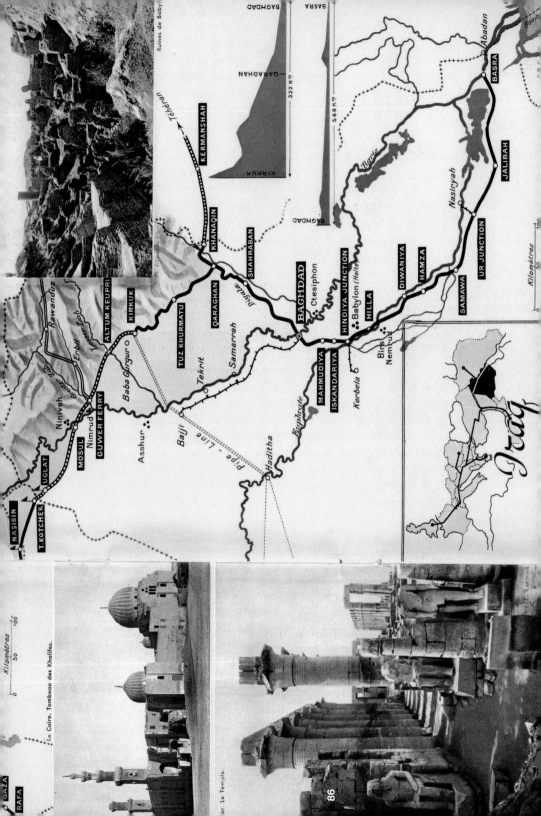

Iraq

BAGHDAD

BASRA

KERMANSHAH

KHANAQIN

SHAHRABAN

QARAGHAN

KIRKUK

ALTUM KEUPRI

TUZ KHURMATU

GUWER FERRY

MOSUL

NASIBIN

T.KOTCHEK

UGLAT

Rawanduz

Erbil

Ninveh

Nimrud

Asshur

Bajji

Teknit

Haditha

Pipe-Line

Samarrah

Diyala

Tigris

Euphrate

Kerbela

Birs
Nemrud

MAHMUDIYA

ISKANDARIYA

HINDIYA JUNCTION

Babylon (Halte)

Ctesiphon

HILLA

DIWANIYA

HAMZA

SAMAWA

UR JUNCTION

Nasiryah

JALIBAH

Abadan

Bombay

GAZA

RAFA

Kilomètres

0   50   100

Baba Gurgur

Upper Zab

Lower Zab

Greater Zab

Téhéran

QARAGHAN

KIRKUK

BAGHDAD

322 KM

569 KM

Ruines de Baby.

Kilomètres

Le Caire. Tombeau des Khalifes.

Le Temple.

86

1887

THE CANADIAN

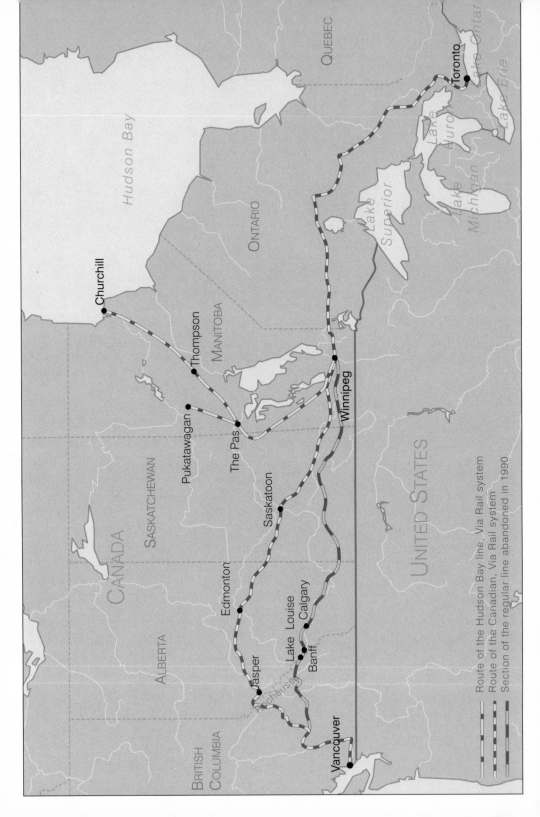

Route of the Hudson Bay line, Via Rail system

Route of the Canadian, Via Rail system

Section of the regular line abandoned in 1990

In the last three decades of the nineteenth century the young Dominion of Canada, the constitution of which had been ratified by the British Parliament in 1867, effectively existed only in name. At this time most of the white settler population was concentrated in the east of the country, with the rest of the vast territory remaining largely beyond the reach of Ottawa's control. As yet the settlers had made no inroads into the immense interior. Beyond the barrier of the Rocky Mountains, a few thousand settlers lived in isolation in British Columbia on the Pacific coast. Far from confident that they would put up much resistance to any American attempts at annexation, in 1870 Sir John A. MacDonald, the first Canadian Prime Minister, made an undertaking to build a railway line to link British Columbia to the rest of Canada. Rash though this promise was, it did succeed in persuading the settlers on the Pacific coast to join the Dominion.

Virtually nothing ensued. The route of the future line came up against the formidable stumbling block of the Rockies, then still largely unmapped. The dubious profitability of the line, traversing as it did uninhabited regions that were "ice-bound for seven months of the year" failed to attract potential investors. And the Manitoba Indian population would stop at nothing to prevent the construction of this new manifestation of arbitrary colonial power. All attempts to unlock the situation ended in failure, feelings became heated, British Columbia threatened in exasperation to secede from the Dominion, private investment gave rise to allegations of bribery of government officials, and in 1873 the MacDonald government fell. The project remained in the doldrums until MacDonald was re-elected five years later. In 1881 the Ottawa government entrusted the building and running of the line to the Canadian Pacific Railway (CPR), incorporated in 1872. Miraculously the project at last got seriously under way, and on 7 November 1885 the famous "last spike" of the line was driven. It was to be another year, however, before trains could start running: there were still stretches of ballast to be laid, stations had yet to be built, and in the west avalanches had already destroyed parts of the line, leaving urgent repair work to be done.

At this stage, the trans-Canadian railway was above all a massive financial black hole. It needed to made profitable, and quickly. The CPR lost no time in launching a major promotional campaign to encourage new immigrants to come to the Canadian West and buy land there. Under the slogan "Ready Made Farms in Western Canada" it offered lots for sale on the 10 million hectares (25 million acres) that the government had granted to the company alongside the railway tracks. The company's other marketing masterstroke came from its president, the multi-talented William Cornelius Van Horne. Impressed by the huge popularity of the Swiss Alps among the elite of international high society, he determined to capitalize on this vogue by promoting the Rockies as the "Canadian Alps." Famously remarking, "If we can't export the scenery, we'll import the tourists," he embarked on a campaign to woo the cosmopolitan clientele of the luxury trains of Europe.

The first passenger train heading for the west coast pulled out of Montreal at eight o'clock on the evening of 28 June 1886, to arrive at Port Moody (some 20km from Vancouver) at noon on 4 July. The line was then the longest in the world and also, as Van Horne had been determined it should be, one of the most comfortable. Even in second class and the "colonist cars" laid on for new settlers of limited means, the ride was said to be a comfortable one. The first-class accommodation, meanwhile, offered a level of luxury well above international standards of the time. In the restaurant cars, meanwhile, the opulence of the fittings—marquetry paneling, button-back leather seats, and fine crystal and silver—was complemented by cordon bleu cuisine that varied with the landscape, featuring local produce such as trout from the St. Lawrence River, Fraser River salmon, and game from the plains. As the train reached the Rockies, however, things took a turn for the worse. Too hastily laid, the track was lacking in tunnels to ease some of the sharper inclines, and the locomotives hurtled down gradients that were twice as steep as the generally accepted norm. In these conditions the restaurant cars effectively became unusable, as crockery, glasses and cutlery went flying and the service was reduced to an undignified scramble. The tremendous weight of the dining cars increased the overall weight of the trains to a dangerous degree, moreover. Eventually a solution was hit upon: the restaurant cars were uncoupled and left at the bottom of inclines, and new "dining stations" were built to take their place. Constructed as they were in the most vertiginous positions, these places of refreshment not only catered for passengers who had been deprived of their restaurant car, but also offered the most splendid views. They were to prove the genesis of the Canadian Pacific hotels.

Picturesque and gaily colored Swiss-style chalets were replaced in time by imposing edifices in a monumental style that was a combination of Tudor manor house,

Renaissance chateau and Scottish baronial castle. These ultimately sprang up along the line's entire length. In the magnificent palace hotels of Alberta, at Banff Springs or Lake Louise, perched above snowy valleys or on the shores of pine-fringed lakes, the railway's wealthy British and Canadian passengers found a sybaritic welcome to rival Singapore or Bombay. Here bear hunts took the place of tiger hunts, and afterwards guests would find the same indispensable high tea to the accompaniment of the usual newspapers. The towns that grew up and flourished along the line also offered their own grand railway hotels in what came to be known as the "chateau style." Vancouver, which soon toppled Port Moody to become the western terminus of the Canadian Pacific, was the site of the first urban railway hotel in 1887. In Quebec, where passengers disembarked from their transatlantic liners, the majestic Chateau Frontenac—flagship of the Canadian Pacific hotels—was built overlooking the St Lawrence River in 1893.

A mari usque ad mare (from sea to sea) was the national motto chosen by the European founders of Canada. It also describes the route of the Canadian Pacific Railway, as it transported a whole world of travelers from one extremity of the country to the other: kings and prime ministers;

lords and duchesses; climbers and adventurers; fishermen, huntsmen and trappers; investors and tourists; globetrotters en route to Asia and even stowaways such as Jack London, who in 1894 traveled the line from east to west hidden beneath a carriage.

Another line, this time run by the Canadian National Railways (CNR), was later built to the north, passing through Edmonton and Jasper. Since the 1990s, this is the only stretch of line across western Canada still to have a trans-continental passenger service (now run by VIA Rail), served three times weekly by the Canadian railroad. Sad though it is that there is now no scheduled service to destinations as glorious as Banff and Lake Louise (apart from the luxury Rocky Mountaineer tourist train), there is some consolation in the fact that the carriages built for the Canadian Pacific in 1955, have been restored and refurbished, and can now be seen crossing the great plains of Manitoba and Saskatchewan, the sun glinting on their sleek stainless steel flanks.

England is determined to hold on to her North American possessions for two reasons: firstly because her national pride allows her to do nothing that might favour any ventures aimed at annexation; and secondly because she has just built a railway that traverses the entire breadth of the Canadian continent, from the Atlantic to the Pacific.

This railway runs parallel to the American railway that links the two oceans some one hundred leagues further south; but the Canadian route seems set to usurp the position of its American rival. Indeed, it now offers the shortest and most direct route from Europe to the Far East; the new railway, known as the "Grand Trunk," therefore seems destined to future greatness.

PHILIPPE DESCHAMPS, 1900

88 | Near Lake Louise, on the former route of the Canadian along the Canadian Pacific Railway, in 1989. On 15 January 1990, the Canadian set off on its last journey on its original CPR route, via Calgary, Lake Louise and Banff, among other spectacular wonders of nature. Though it no longer sees the Canadian, the route is now the Rocky Mountaineer tourist train.

101 | Château Frontenac, Quebec, viewed from the St Lawrence River c.1900. The hotel, which opened its doors in 1893 to welcome Canadian Pacific passengers as they disembarked from their transatlantic steam crossings, quickly established a reputation as one of the finest in Canada. Its turreted combination of Renaissance château and Scottish baronial became the definitive example of the "château style," henceforth de rigueur for all Canadian Pacific hotels. Later elevated to become the Canadian "national style," until the Second World War it set the tone for all Canadian buildings anxious to present a dignified exterior.

102 | A night view of the Canadian. The rolling stock in current use consists of the refurbished stainless steel carriages built for the Canadian Pacific Railway in 1955.

103 | The Canadian at Capreol Station, Ontario, 2002. At the back of the train is a Park car, an observation car reserved for passengers traveling in the luxury Silver and Blue class.

104-105 | Internal and external views of a Vista Dome on the Canadian. The idea of observation cars with glass domes offering panoramic views and accessible to passengers in all classes was developed in America. The earliest examples were on the California Zephyr (see p.244).

106 | Jasper Station was built in 1926 to replace a former Grand Trunk Station that burned down during the winter of 1924-25, its architecture and materials chosen to harmonize with its majestic mountain surroundings. Owned since 2001 by Parks Canada, restored and refurbished, it is now known as Jasper Heritage Railway Station.

107 | A flock of bighorn sheep in the Jasper National Park, Alberta, viewed from the present transcontinental route of the Canadian in 2002.

108-109 | The Canadian heading westwards. Although the Rockies presented the most formidable obstacle to the building of the track, water could also pose enormous difficulties. In some places the line had to be built on stilts or even on floating timber rafts.

110-111 | Scenes on the Great North line, heading for Churchill. In addition to the Canadian, VIA Rail also offers a tourist route between Winnipeg and the port of Churchill, Manitoba, on the shores of Hudson Bay. The train, called the Hudson Bay, is the only means of reaching these remote parts by land. When winter hits

Birth of a transcontinental railway: on 7 November 1885, Donald A. Smith drove the fabled "last spike" into the track at Craigellachie, British Columbia, so joining the western and eastern sections of the line.

Navvies working on the track in the 1880s, when it was still under construction.

this sub-Arctic region, railroad men wielding sledgehammers have to smash off the thick layer of ice that encases the undercarriage of the trains. For lovers of the great outdoors who fancy a spot of walking, hunting or dog-sledding, the Hudson Bay offers an unusual feature: duly warned in advance, the engineer will stop to let them off at any point on the line, regardless of whether there is a station or halt.

112 ı A stag contemplates the passing of the Canadian in the Rocky Mountains.

113 ı The interior of the Bullet Lounge in a Park car, the observation car at the rear of the Canadian, 1989. With its wrap-around windows, panoramic views, comfortable armchairs and attentive service (with tea, coffee and newspapers constantly available), this lounge is reserved for Silver and Blue class passengers.

114 ı Vancouver Station, c.1900, showing the "château style" as enthusiastically adopted by Canadian Pacific stations. Competition with the United States stimulated Canadian loyalty to this somber, monumental style, in stark contrast to the neo-classicism favored by American railway architecture. The fledgling nation was eager to assert its autonomy.

115-117 ı The Canadian in the Rockies. As soon as the line had been built, Van Horne realized that he had to find a way of protecting the track from rock falls and

The Notman brothers were official photographers to the Canadian Pacific Railway. This photograph shows the specially adapted carriage that was reserved for them (behind the engine), with its own dark room.

Far left: A 1947
poster by Peter Ewart
for the Canadian
Pacific Railway.
Left: The station at
Lake Louise, c.1900.

I was in Ottawa, bound west over the Canadian Pacific. Three thousand miles of that road stretched before me; it was the fall of the year, and I had to cross Manitoba and the Rocky Mountains. I could expect "crimpy" weather, and every moment of delay increased the frigid hardships of the journey. Furthermore, I was disgusted. ...Furthermore, my disgust had been heightened by the one day I had spent in Ottawa trying to get an outfit of clothing for my long journey. ...At six I quit work and headed for the railroad yards. ...When I arrived at the depot, I found, much to my disgust, a bunch of at least twenty tramps that were waiting to ride out the blind baggages of the overland. Now two or three tramps on the blind baggage are all right. They are inconspicuous. But a score! That meant trouble. No train-crew would ever let all of us ride.

JACK LONDON, 1907

avalanches. Adopting a solution already adopted by the Americans on the Central Pacific Railway, he built solid wooden avalanche shelters to protect sections of line that were most vulnerable. In 1916 the 8-km double-track Connaught tunnel was opened under Rogers Pass (west of Lake Louise), replacing 32km of single track that included 7.6km of avalanche shelters.

118 | The Canadian in the Rocky Mountains, on its former route on the Canadian Pacific Railway near Banff, Alberta, in the 1980s. It was near here that workmen found the hot springs around which, in 1887, Canada's first national park would be created (another brainchild of Van Horne); originally called the Rocky Mountains Park, it later became the Banff National Park.

119 | Road and railway together snake through a pass in the Rockies, 1920s.

120 | View of the Bow River from one of the rooms in the Banff Springs Hotel, 1988. Marilyn Monroe stayed in the hotel when filming *The River of No Return* here in 1953.

121 | The Banff Springs Hotel rising majestically among the dramatic mountain scenery at the confluence of the Spray and Bow rivers, c. 1900. Opened in 1888 with the 250 rooms and the ultimate in modern comforts, Banff Springs was described in Canadian Pacific brochures as "the finest hotel on the North American continent."

122 | The Canadian Pacific at

The Lake Louise electric tramway, which ran from the station to the hotel in the 1920s.

Sicamous, British Columbia, in the 1920s. Less ambitious than Banff Springs, the Canadian Pacific hotel at Sicamous, built in 1894, offered a relaxed atmosphere and a range of outdoor sports and activities.

123 ɪ Staff from the Château Lake Louise hotel, Alberta, sweeping the ice in preparation for guests wishing to go skating, 1988. At

Lake Louise, the magnificent natural setting and the increasing numbers of visitors it attracted persuaded Canadian Pacific to construct a branch line to the hotel to provide access from the main line. This was completed in 1891, whereupon work began on the building of a single-storey timber hotel to accommodate the flood of visitors.

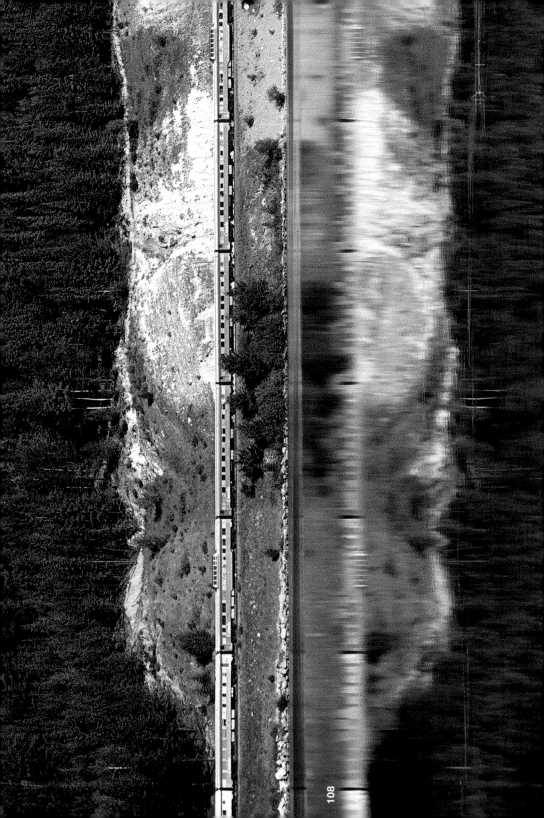

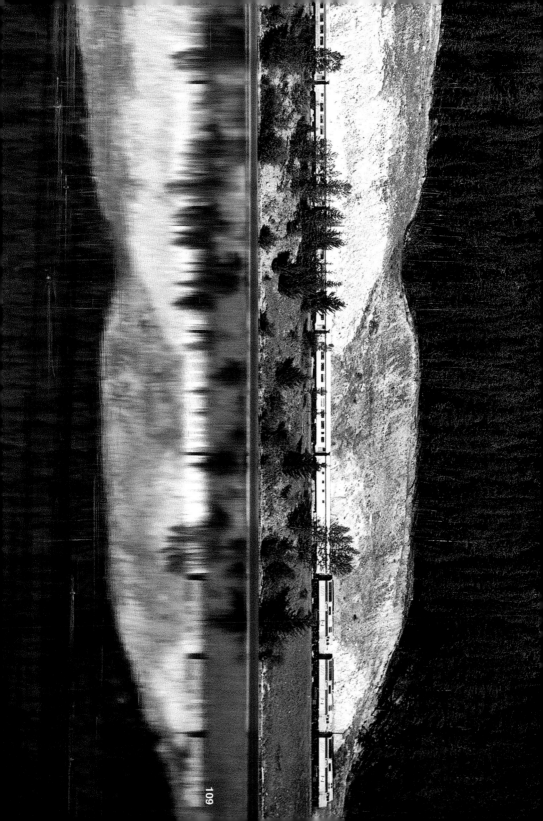

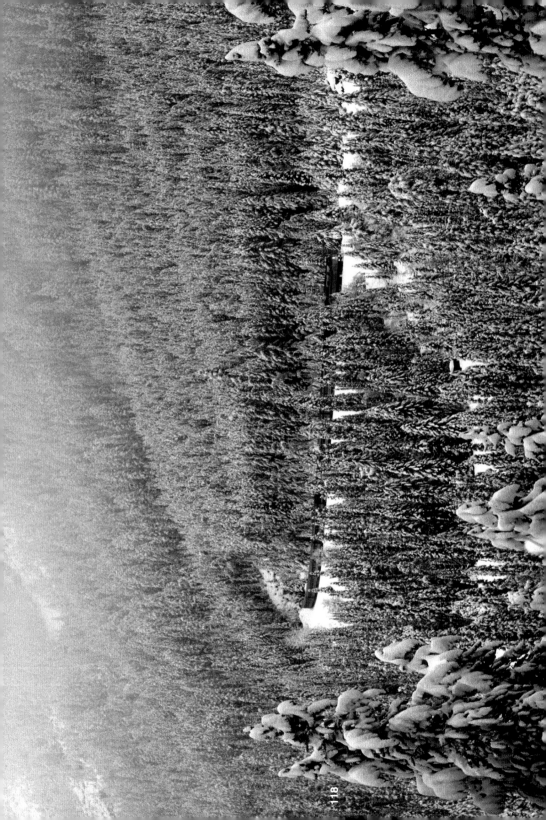

The Trans-Siberian Railway

1900

By the 1870s Russia already had railways. The line from St Petersburg to Moscow had been in service since 1851, and to judge from accounts by contemporary travelers, Russian railway travel was an extremely comfortable affair. The main stations were elegant buildings boasting welcoming waiting rooms and well-stocked buffets. Commodious carriages were both taller and broader than their European counterparts. On his travels through Russia, the French writer Théophile Gautier was enchanted by the country's railways. He was particularly impressed by the arrangement of the carriages en enfilade so as to form virtually self-contained apartments, preceded by an anteroom containing washing and toilet facilities, and furnished with divan beds or "well sprung and well upholstered wing chairs." Equally, the efficient heating provided by roaring wood stoves, which even during the grueling winters maintained a temperature inside the carriages of between 15 and 16 degrees Fahrenheit, was a cause of great satisfaction to him. What he did not know was that these stoves, combined with the quilted and cushioned upholstery, posed a constant risk of fire. A partial remedy to this problem was seized upon, and heating was removed altogether from third-class carriages, where the wretched passengers were abandoned to their freezing fate until the authorities could think of a better solution.

The other major drawback of the Russian railway network was that travelers wishing to journey to the east had to go by sleigh in winter, and for the rest of the year were decanted into the notorious tarantass, an all-terrain wickerwork contraption slung between two birch poles linking the axles, of which Count K. K. Pahlen, in his account of his Mission to Turkestan, 1908–09, observed: "After the comfort of the saloon railway-carriage which had conveyed our party to Kabul-sai the transition to this mode of locomotion was something of a shock. … The tarantass went bumping up and down like a boat on a rough sea and the only thing we, the unfortunate passengers, could do was to sit tight and try to avoid being hurled out." As the furs that formed Siberia's principal wealth could satisfactorily be transported to Moscow in the traditional ways, the authorities saw no reason to build a railway link between Moscow and this remote and inhospitable region.

But gradually ideas began to change. The railway line started to snake eastwards to Chelyabinsk; Siberia began to yield up its mineral riches; and the Russian empire stretched eastwards with the acquisition of Vladivostok. And above and beyond all these factors, Russia found itself caught in an ineluctable pincer movement of modernization to both the west and the east. To the west lay the United States, which had boasted a transcontinental railway since 1869, and Europe, where the railway network was growing ever denser; and to the east lay Japan which, little changed from the middle ages to the mid-nineteenth century, was now catching up with breathtaking speed, and in 1872 inaugurated a railway linking Tokyo and Yokohama. So it was that Tsar Alexander III eventually took the decision to embark on the Herculean task of building a railway line across Siberia, from Moscow to Vladivostok, with branch lines to Port Arthur and Peking. His son and heir, Grand Duke Nikolai, laid the foundation stone for the new trans-Siberian railway, at Vladivostok on 19 May 1891. The work (which was to take a quarter of a century) started simultaneously in both east and west. The chief difficulties lay not in the terrain but rather in the implacable cold (with the land sometimes staying frozen as late as July); the massive quantities of snow; the mighty rivers that flowed across the region; and water everywhere. The birch forests of the taiga were waterlogged to an impressive depth, requiring the building of innumerable embankments and low bridges to raise the railway track above the level of the water. To cap it all, the distances between supply stations were huge and local labor virtually impossible to find: a problem that was remedied by press-ganging convicts and exiles into service, dangling before them the promise of remission of their sentences.

By these means, the track grew at the highly satisfactory rate of 600 kilometers annually. And already it was providing a return on its considerable investment, not in first or second-class ticket sales, but in the teeming masses of third class, swelled by a growing tide of immigrants. In 1892, the Siberian gold rush attracted 60,000 hopeful souls, rising to 200,000 in 1899. By 1900, it was indeed possible to travel from Europe to Vladivostok by train—but only with the help of river navigation, as the line was not yet finished. When they reached the banks of the rivers Chilka and Amur, for example, passengers had to detrain on to boats for the 2,240 kilometers that separated Sretensk from Khabarovsk, 900 kilometers north of Vladivostok. In its western section, meanwhile, the Trans-Siberian came up against the mammoth obstacle of Lake Baikal, where two new and enormous ice-breaking ferries, built in a British shipyard, shipped the train in its entirety across the world's largest freshwater lake. Work started on a new section of track to skirt round the lake's southern end in 1899, to be completed in 1904. At this period it also became clear that the earlier sections of track required attention: standards had been sacrificed for the sake of speed, and a mere 25 cm

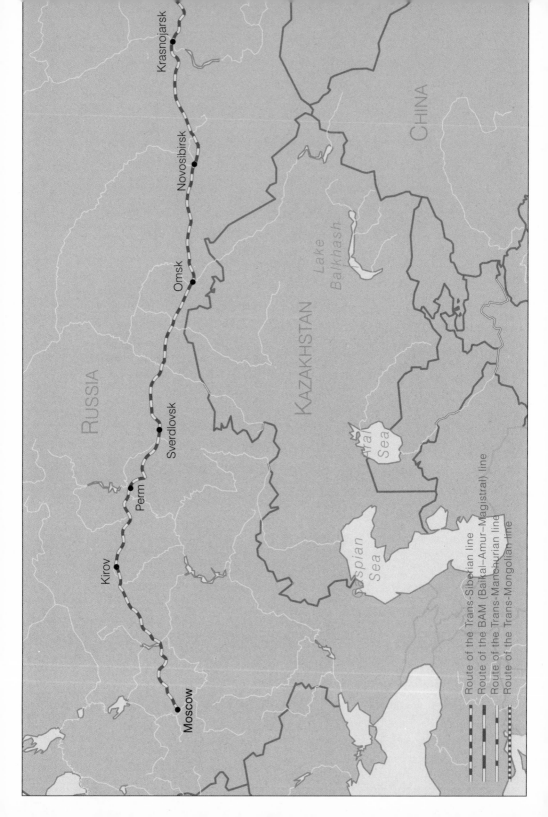

Krasnojarsk

Novosibirsk

Omsk

Sverdlovsk

Perm

Kirov

Moscow

RUSSIA

KAZAKHSTAN

CHINA

Lake Balkhash

Aral Sea

Caspian Sea

Route of the Trans-Siberian line
Route of the BAM (Baikal–Amur–Magistral) line
Route of the Trans-Manchurian line
Route of the Trans-Mongolian line

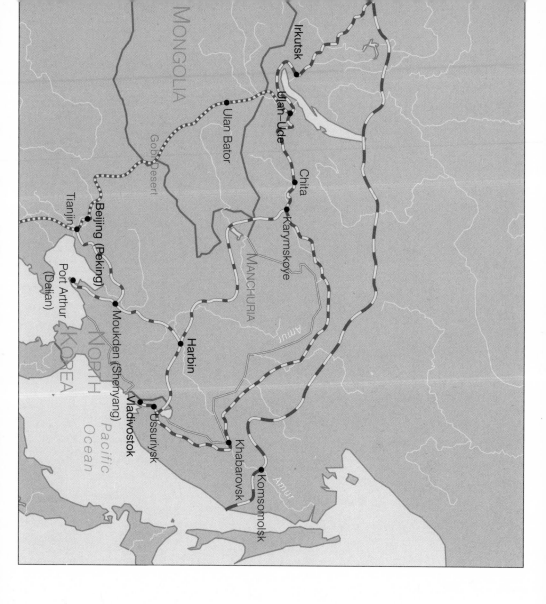

of ballast had been laid instead of the regulation 47cm, with the track even being laid on bare earth in places; the sleepers, which had not been treated before being laid, were rotting; there were no stations with loops to relieve congestion on the single-track line; and the tunnels through the Sayan Mountains, with their steep inclines and dangerous bends, needed replacing. Although it was considered as finished by around 1916, the Trans-Siberian was in fact still under continuous reconstruction.

Georges Nagelmackers (see "The Orient Express") was keen to launch a handsome luxury train on the new trans-Siberian line, but the Russian authorities took a dim view of this attempt at foreign interference. Russia already boasted its own luxury trains, moreover, and well before the Compagnie Internationale des Wagons-Lits fitted out the first French presidential train for President Félix Faure, Tsar Alexander II already had a special imperial train of eleven carriages, equipped with electricity and telephones.

Undeterred, at the Paris Exposition Universelle in 1900, Nagelmackers displayed a magnificent Trans-Siberian train, though it was never destined to run on the Russian railway. Harassment, sabotage, and the humiliation of being obliged to add a second-class carriage in order to render the train less ostentatious, ensured that the Trans-Siberian of the

Compagnie Internationale des Wagons-Lits would never have the monopoly on the line. A second Trans-Siberian Express, operated in parallel by the Russian state, claimed all the best timetable slots for itself, and from 1917 the Wagons-Lits train was discontinued.

In 1917 the Bolsheviks confiscated the Wagons-Lits rolling stock, and the company managed to rescue only a dozen or so carriages out of a total of 160. Henceforth the Trans-Siberian Express was resolutely and exclusively Russian, in due course appearing in a luxury form of which the Soviet Union could be justly proud. Lenin himself was known to succumb to the dissolute opulence of the enigmatic blue train which, when it stopped in any station, was strictly out of bounds to members of the proletariat. This railway line built by the tsars remained the backbone of the USSR, together with the Trans-Manchurian, the Trans-Mongolian (retracing the route of the tea caravans), and more recently the BAM (Baikal-Amur Mainline), to the north of the original line. Today's railway travelers can still follow the classic route from Moscow to Vladivostok. The aluminum and Plexiglas Rossiya, the only named Moscow Vladivostok express on the Trans-Siberian railway, offers an epic 9,000 kilometer journey lasting seven nights and six days, and crossing no fewer than seven different time zones.

AGENCE DE LA C^{IE} DES WAGONS-LITS A PÉKIN. ~ RUE DES LÉGATIONS

GRAND HOTEL DES WAGONS LITS PEKING

On leaving Perm the railway line heads north, passing the iron smelting works at Motavilikia before following the left bank of the Kama and soon after crossing the Chusovaya. This line from Perm to Ekaterinburg, a 500-kilometer stretch, was opened in 1878, and work is now continuing to extend it as far as Tyumen. In a year's time, trains will run from Ekaterinburg to Tyumen (and soon, in three or four years perhaps, the great Siberian railway from Kazan to Irkutsk will be built, so cutting the journey by a good half). The carriages are most comfortable and even luxurious. A novelty for me was the sight of couchettes above the seats themselves. I am not explaining myself well: halfway up the carriage, which is relatively high, the back rest of the seat may be pulled down to form a foldaway couchette on which one may easily lie; thus we sleep one above the other.

ALBERT ROUSSY, 1883

124 | A Siberian snowscape glimpsed through frost patterns on a Trans-Siberian carriage window.
137 | An engine gets ready to pull a train on the BAM route, east of Bratsk.
138 | Place Tworskoi, Moscow, photochrome, 1895.
139 | In the run-up to the launch of its Trans-Siberian Express, the Compagnie Internationale des

Wagons-Lits organized a maiden journey—at greatly reduced prices—in 1898. An advertisement to this effect was placed in European newspapers, but curiously not a single intrepid soul responded, and not a single reservation was taken.
140 | The large drawing room in carriage 724, one of the Trans-Siberian carriages displayed by

the Compagnie Internationale des Wagons-Lits at the Paris Exposition Universelle of 1900. Carriage 724 also boasted a bathroom (complete with bath) in green sycamore wood and a "cycling room" in which travelers could stretch their legs on the journey across Russia.
141 | Brochure produced by the Compagnie Internationale des

Wagons-Lits to advertise the presence of the Trans-Siberian Express at the 1900 Exposition Universelle. Visitors could dine in the carriages on display, while to complete the illusion a panoramic vista (painted on canvas by the scenic painters of the Paris Opéra) slid by outside the windows, complete with scenes of snow-capped mountains, railway

132

In the somber and desolate train station, the station master, wearing a red cap, hurried out when the bell chimed announcing the arrival of the train. Dressed in furs, he protected himself against the cold by hiding his face. Then when the bell had tolled three times according to regulations, the train pulled out of the station and continued on its journey through the vast white plain. It was very much the Siberia that has been described by the novelists.

JOHN FORSTER FRASER, 1902

tracks, dramatic skies, traditional wooden isbas and sleighs.

142 | On the platform at a Siberian station on the Trans-Siberian route. Photo Turot, verascope, c.1905.

143 | A typical small station on the Trans-Siberian line. Photo Turot, verascope, c.1905.

144 | Irkutsk Station, terminus of the western section of the Trans-Siberian route, opened in 1898.

Photo Chemin-Dupontès, verascope, c.1911.

145 | View of the Siberian taiga from the windows of a BAM sleeping car.

146 | Inside a BAM sleeping compartment, between Tynda and Severobaïkalsk (on the northern shore of Lake Baikal).

147 | 147 The Trans-Siberian on the shores of Lake Baikal.

Photo Kritch, verascope, c.1905. Until this time trains were floated across Lake Baikal on board two ice-breaking ferries specially commissioned from a British shipyard: the *Baikal* and the *Angara*.

148-149 | Vladivostok, future eastern terminus of the Trans-Siberian route, in the 1880s.

150-151 | Trans-Siberian and

Rossiya dining cars in Vladivostok Station, 2004.

152 | Dining car on the Vladivostok-Harbin line, 1920s. Originally a Wagons-Lits passenger car, this carriage was transformed into a dining car after the Bolshevik government seized the company's assets in 1917.

153 | Left: Brochure in oriental style advertising the far-eastern

As we watched, the contrast between the cold air outside and the warm air inside began to sketch faint quicksilver sprigs and branches on the window of the door, which rapidly intertwined and spread out into broad, leafy shapes, forming an enchanted forest. …Nothing could be more beautiful than these sprays and arabesques, these lacy filigrees of ice traced so delicately by winter's finger. …Yet after you have gazed at them for an hour, you begin to grow impatient with this veil of white embroidery that stops you from seeing or being seen. …In France we would simply have pulled the window down; but in Russia this would have been an imprudence of potentially fatal consequences: the cold, constantly lying in wait for its prey, would have stretched its monstrous polar bear paw into the carriage and slapped us in the face with its claws.

THÉOPHILE GAUTHIER, 1859

The station at Polomochnaia in Siberia, seen from the Trans-Siberian Express. Photo by Chemin-Dupontès, 14 March 1903.

route of the Wagons-Lits Trans-Siberian Express. Right: The moderne-style saloon car of the Trans-Manchurian.

154 ı During a halt on the Trans-Manchurian line, a group of local Chinese musicians gives an impromptu concert on the track. Phot Zo d'Axa, verascope, c.1908.

155 ı Waiting area in the station at Nancha, on the Trans-Manchurian line.

156 ı Peking (Beijing) Station, c.1900: arrival of the Trans-Manchurian.

157 ı Just a few miles outside Peking by rail, passengers could visit the Great Wall, 1928.

158 ı Mouth of a railway tunnel, Peking, 1928.

159 ı The Trans-Mongolian crossing the Gobi Desert.

134

Three days later, I took the train with two traveling companions for the capital of outer Siberia. …Still climbing through fields up the Siufun valley, we reached the major center of Nikolskoye. Only the tall scaffolding of a cathedral under construction rose above an expanse of low wooden houses, broadly scattered over the plain. A motley crowd jostled each other on the platform: Russian soldiers, Siberian peasants, Koreans and Chinese. Nikolskoye is the point where the eastern Trans-Manchurian branches off from the Ussuri line, and troops flock to it from all directions. Around the station there has sprung up a small town of offices and workshops. It is immediately noticeable that the Trans-Manchurian locomotives are larger and more powerful than those of the Ussuri line, built to go faster on sturdier track.

M. G. WEULERSSE, 1901

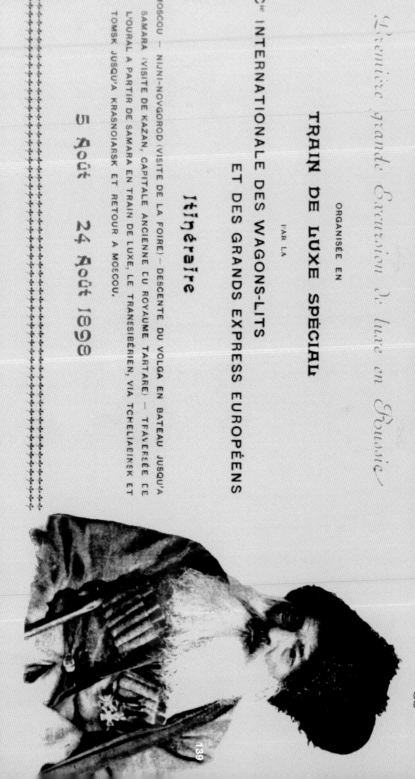

Le Transsibérien

Première grande Excursion de luxe en Russie

Cⁱᵉ INTERNATIONALE DES WAGONS-LITS
ET DES GRANDS EXPRESS EUROPÉENS

TRAIN DE LUXE SPÉCIAL

ORGANISÉE EN

PAR LA

Itinéraire

MOSCOU — NIJNI-NOVGOROD (VISITE DE LA FOIRE).— DESCENTE DU VOLGA EN BATEAU JUSQU'A SAMARA (VISITE DE KAZAN, CAPITALE ANCIENNE DU ROYAUME TARTARE).— TFAVERÉE CE L'OURAL A PARTIR DE SAMARA EN TRAIN DE LUXE, LE TRANSSIBÉRIEN, VIA TCHELIAEINSK ET TOMSK JUSQU'A KRASNOIARSK ET RETOUR A MOSCOU.

5 Août   24 Août 1898

139

РОССИЯ
ОМСК-ВЛАДИВОСТОК

РОССИЯ

084
1084

THE UGANDA RAILWAY OR LUNATIC LINE

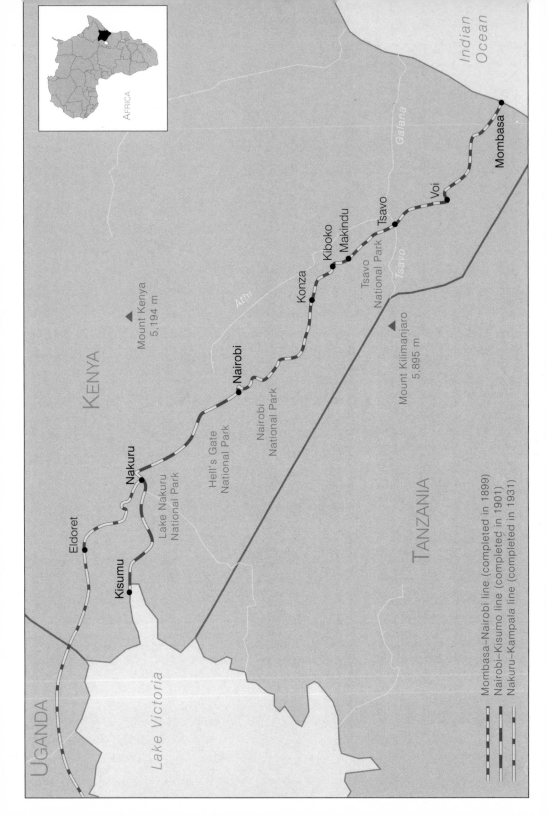

AFRICA

Indian
Ocean

Mombasa

Galana

Voi

Tsavo

Makindu

Kiboko

Tsavo National Park

Tsavo

Konza

Mount Kilimanjaro
5,895 m

Athi

Nairobi

KENYA

Mount Kenya
5,194 m

Nairobi
National Park

Hell's Gate
National Park

Nakuru

TANZANIA

Lake Nakuru
National Park

Eldoret

Kisumu

UGANDA

Lake Victoria

Mombasa–Nairobi line (completed in 1899)
Nairobi–Kisumo line (completed in 1901)
Nakuru–Kampala line (completed in 1931)

What it will cost no words can express;
What is its object no brain can suppose;
Where it will start from no one can guess;
Where it is going nobody knows;
What is the use of it none can conjecture;
What it will carry there's none can define;
And in spite of George Curzon's superior lecture,
It clearly is naught but a lunatic line.

Readers of the London Magazine, which published this prescient snatch of doggerel in 1896, would have been left in no doubt as the controversial nature of this "lunatic" project. Indeed, reactions to the recently started scheme to build a railway line from the Indian Ocean port of Mombasa in Kenya to Lake Victoria, work on which had recently started, divided Parliament and the nation. The Conservatives, including Lord Curzon, Viceroy of India from 1898, were determined that the line should be forced through at any price. Not only would it give Uganda access to the sea, but it would also strengthen the British Empire's hold on the eastern half of Africa. Their Liberal opponents, by contrast, were equally implacably opposed to the scheme: fraught with danger, burdened with crippling expense and

based on the flagrant expropriation of Maasai lands, there was only one word for it: lunatic!

But still, work had started—even if only at a snail's pace. By the end of the first year, the railway had penetrated a derisory 40 kilometers (24 miles) into the interior. First it had to cross the parched Taru Plain, where every last drop of water for the construction camps had to brought in by train from Mombasa. Already the men were exhausted and worn down by dysentery, and the sleepers they laid one day would be devoured by termites the next. By March 1898 the track had reached the banks of the River Tsavo. No sooner had work started on a bridge to carry the railway across the river, however, then the men downed tools and fled in their hundreds. The Tsavo camp, it transpired, was haunted on a daily basis by two man-eating lions: powerful beasts whose roars echoed eerily through the night air, and who in the space of nine months were to devour no fewer than 140 porters and other workers. Great fires were lit around the encampment, thorny palisades were thrown up, traps were sunk, but all to no avail. Undeterred, Ghost and Shadow, as the man-eaters came to be known, continued to terrorize the workforce, gaining a reputation for supernatural invincibility. Yet work had to continue, whatever the cost: the chief engineer, Captain (later Lt. Colonel) John Patterson, made it his mission to hunt down the killers, eventually succeeding in shooting the first (measuring three meters, or nearly ten feet, from nose to tail) on 9 December 1898, followed by the second three weeks later.

A year later the bridge was finished. Duty done, Patterson set about turning a tidy profit from his thrilling adventure, writing four successful books and addressing conferences throughout the world. Shrewdly, in 1924 he offered the skins of the Tsavo lions for sale to the Field Museum of Chicago, who agreed to pay a handsome price for them. Lions continued to threaten the progress of the line, however, and these were far from the last deaths they were to cause. Perhaps the most spectacular attack took place at the station at Kima, where Police Superintendent C.H. Ryall was slumbering in his private carriage when a lion burst in, dragged him through the window and made off with him into the bush. The unfortunate Ryall's carriage is now on display in Nairobi Railway Museum. Altogether, the railway was to claim over 2,500 lives, with a further 6,000 injuries. To cap it all, the local populations of gazelle, zebra and antelope were decimated by disease at this

period, driving starving lions, deprived of their usual prey, to look elsewhere.

This epidemic also had a devastating effect on the Maasai people, spreading famine among populations already suffering from an onslaught of problems, including internal fighting. As far as the pragmatic British were concerned, the weakened state of the Maasai offered a now or never opportunity to push through a right of passage for their railway line. In granting permission the Maasai were in fact only bowing to the inevitable: had not their mythology spoken since the dawn of time of the "iron snake" that would one day insinuate itself into their lands and destroy their lives and culture?

In May 1899, the railway construction workers set up a base camp and supply depot, called simply "Mile 327," on a patch of highland crossed by a stream known to the local Maasai as *Uaso Nairobi*, meaning "cold water". Soon the administrative offices of the railway company were transferred from Mombasa to this new settlement, to be joined by the headquarters of the British colonial administration: thus the town known as Nairobi was born. In December 1901 the line finally reached the shores of Lake Victoria, at a spot then named Port Florence, afterwards known as Kisumu. But the work was still not complete: permanent viaducts were still needed to carry the railway across the monumental terrain and bridge the dizzying chasms of the Highlands and the Rift Valley. By 1903 the line was operational from the Indian Ocean to Lake Victoria, a distance of almost a thousand kilometers. The link with the Ugandan capital Kampala would not be completed until 1931.

The railway had opened up new and potentially highly profitable vistas for the colonial administration. From 1910 or thereabouts, European settlers flocked to this new El Dorado, setting up the first farms and coffee plantations around Nairobi, in Naivasha and, as Karen Blixen remembered (under her nom de plume Isak Dinesen) in Out of Africa, in the Ngong foothills: "I had a farm in Africa, at the foot of the Ngong Hills. The Equator runs across these highlands, a hundred miles to the North, and the farm lay at an altitude of over six thousand feet. In the day-time you felt that you had got high up, near to the sun, but the early mornings and evenings were limpid and restful, and the nights were cold." Now stripped of their fertile lands, the Maasai were soon herded into two reservations flanking the railway line, only to be expelled from the northern reservation a short time later.

So what remains today of this railway that was once the main artery of East Africa? Passenger trains to Kampala are suspended until further notice, but Kenya Railways maintain regular passenger services between Kisumu and Nairobi, and from Nairobi to Mombasa. Delays are all part of the service, and understandably so, as on this single-track line it takes only a derailment in some far-flung spot or a herd of elephant on the track to disrupt the service nationally. Three times a week, night trains run from Nairobi to Mombasa and vice versa. With its couchettes, sleeping compartments and delightfully superannuated dining car—all mahogany paneling, monogrammed silver plate and white-gloved waiters, a beguiling mix of African charm and faded British gentility—the Lunatic Express (as it now tends to be known) remains the preferred means of transport for tourists, despite taking an impressive 14 hours to cover 530 kilometers. Booking ahead is essential, as it is always full. Recently privatized, the railway is now in receipt of substantial World Bank funding in order to regain and maintain its position as a competitive form of transport.

[I have] a very vivid recollection of one particular night when the brutes seized a man from the railway station and brought him close to my camp to devour. I could plainly hear them crunching the bones, and the sound of their dreadful purring filled the air and rang in my ears for days afterwards. The terrible thing was to feel so helpless: it was useless to attempt to go out, as of course the poor fellow was dead.

LT. COL. J. H. PATTERSON,
THE MAN-EATERS OF TSAVO, 1907

160 ı A child balances on the track of the Lunatic Line, a single-track railway running almost a thousand kilometers from the Indian Ocean to Lake Victoria with virtually no junctions. So limited is the service nowadays that pedestrians can use it without fear.

169 ı A locomotive in Mombasa Station during boarding of one of Charles Alluard's scientific expeditions into British East Africa (present-day Kenya), verascope, 1908–09. In its infancy, the Uganda Railway benefited greatly from the equipment and widely adopted methods used by the British to build the railways of the Raj from the 1850s. The first managers and supervisors for the new project were moreover drawn from the highly experienced ranks of the Indian civil service. Both literally and metaphorically, the Uganda Railway was conceived on the model of the Indian railways. The gauge adopted was the meter gauge used on the other side of the Indian Ocean, and in case of emergency fully operational locomotives could be imported from Bombay and pressed into immediate service.

170 ı The train carrying the Alluaud expedition to British East Africa prepares to pull out of Mombasa Station en route for Uganda, verascope, 1908–09. At this time there was not yet a railway link to Uganda (the Nakuru to Kampala line was completed only in 1931), so at Kisumu passengers detrained on to ferries to cross Lake Victoria.

166

The inspection train traveled the long straight on the Taru Desert between mile 59 and 83, at the rate of 30 miles per hour, without seriously interfering with the comforts of our afternoon tea.

INSPECTION REPORT BY C. W. HODSON,
SUPERINTENDING ENGINEER, 1897

171 | Detail of a "Mountain" locomotive at Nairobi station, 1976. Some of the largest and heaviest steam engines in the East African Railways fleet, Mountain locomotives operated only between Nairobi and Mombasa, on the only stretch of line solid enough to support their colossal weight. They were used to pull passenger trains from 1955 (when they were first built) to the late 1960s, when the first diesel locomotives were introduced.

172 | Maintenance work on a steam engine at the Thika depot. In recent years Kenyan steam engines have been brought back into sporadic service on tourist routes, for instance pulling the Steam Safari Trains that, amid dramatic clouds of steam, carry visitors to Kenya's national parks.

173 | Beyer Garratt locomotive 6010 under repair at Nairobi.

174 | Silver plate still sporting the EAR monogram of East African Railways, in the dining car of the Nairobi–Mombasa night train, 1984. Run from its inception by Uganda Railways, the Lunatic Line later became part of the East African Railways network, before passing to Kenya Railways in 1978.

175 | Passing cultivated fields on the Nairobi–Mombasa line, 1984.

176-177 | A herd of wild elephant viewed from the train, somewhere between Nairobi and Mombasa, 1984. On the night train from Mombasa to Nairobi passengers have little chance of seeing such magnificent sights, as the train leaves at seven o'clock in the evening and by the time it reaches Tsavo National Park night has already fallen.

178-179 ı Dining car and wine selection on the Nairobi-Mombasa service, 1984. The charm of spending a night on this service (now known as the Jambo Kenya Deluxe) owes a great deal to the quaintly old-fashioned atmosphere of the dining car, built in Birmingham in the 1950s. The original crockery, cutlery and silverware are still in use, causing major (though well-concealed) headaches for the staff. Lost forks, broken cups and other casualties are never replaced, making it increasingly difficult to amass the full complement for each diner. It is not unknown, consequently, for passengers to be hurried along discreetly so that the staff can hastily retrieve scarce items needed for other diners.

180 ı Charles Alluaud's expedition to British East Africa at Nairobi Station, verascope, 1908-09. Ten years before this

photograph was taken the station did not exist, and Nairobi was still a Maasai watering hole crossed by a small river. It was beside this river that the railway depot was built, and in 1901 the capital of the British Protectorate was transferred from Mombasa to Nairobi, the better to control the interior.

181-182 ı "Mountain" locomotives at the Nairobi depot, September 1976.

183 ı Nairobi Station: unloading the baggage of the Charles Alluaud expedition to British East Africa, verascope, 1908-09.

184-185 ı The single track of the Lunatic Line, making its lonely way across the wastes of the Taru Desert, 1984. Could this be the "iron snake" of Maasai ancestral myth?

186 ı Locomotive taking on wood in the Samburu heartland, photographed in verascope by Alluard, 1904. From here the Lunatic Line headed north towards Mount Kenya. The Samburu is now a National Reserve.

187 ı A stationary Steam Safari Train at Fort Ternan, 22 September 2005. Running a monthly tourist service between Nairobi and Naivasha, the train is drawn by steam locomotive 3020. Here it is taking on some of its daily requirement of around 30,000 liters of water.

188 ı A tourist train pulling out of Moshi in Tanzania, on the branch line from Voi in Kenya, September 1976. Behind it rises the unmistakable silhouette of Mount Kilimanjaro, at the foot of which Moshi lies.

189 ı The Steam Safari Train halted at Kipkelion, 22 September 2005, demonstrating that steam trains are as popular with the local inhabitants as with tourists.

190 ı Maasai warriors at Lumbwa Station, between Nairobi and Lake Victoria, photographed in verascope by Charles Alluaud, c.1904.

191 ı The East African Steam Safari pulls into Chemellil Station, 29 September 2005.

MOUNT KILIMANJARO

19340FT

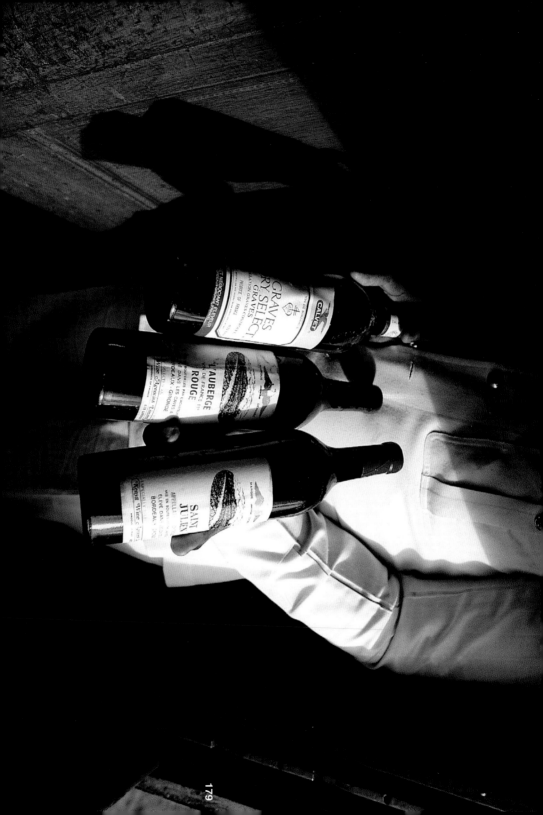

1922

THE TRAIN BLEU

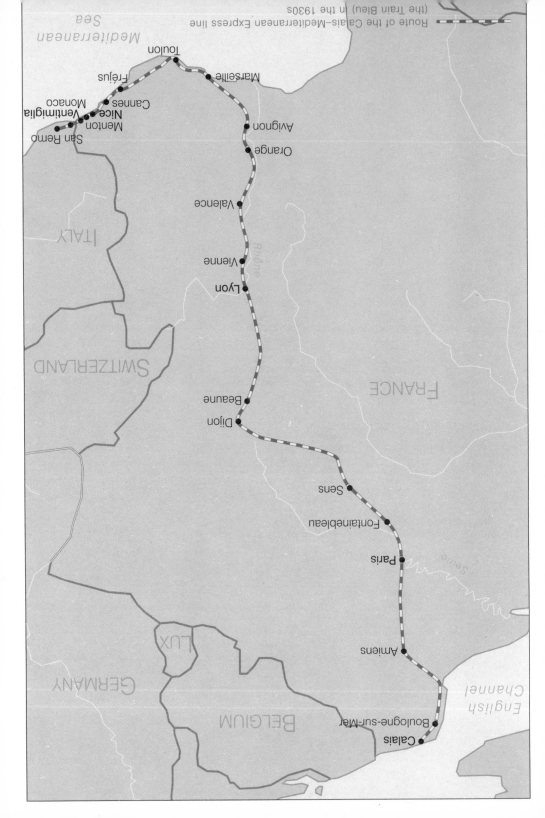

Route of the Calais–Mediterranean Express line (the Train Bleu) in the 1930s

Mediterranean Sea

Toulon
Fréjus
Cannes
Monaco
Ventimiglia
Nice
Menton
San Remo
Marseille
Avignon
Orange
Valence
Vienne
Lyon
Beaune
Dijon
Sens
Fontainebleau
Paris
Amiens
Boulogne-sur-Mer
Calais

ITALY
SWITZERLAND
FRANCE
LUX
GERMANY
BELGIUM

Rhône
Seine

English Channel

The Train Bleu was far from being the only great express train to serve the Riviera. There were more enigmatic conveyances, such as the Calais–Nice–Rome Express, on which passengers stood every chance of rubbing shoulders with a papal nunzio and even in the depths of winter dined on fresh *petits pois* (picked on Corfu, purchased in Brindisi and conveyed to Calais by the Indian Mail). There were more eccentric ones, such as the St Petersburg–Vienna–Nice–Cannes Express, which from 1898 daily disgorged its complement of Middle European aristocrats on the promenades of the Côte d'Azur. And there were even ones more shrouded in mystery, such as the Riviera Express, which from 1900 whisked wealthy passengers from the mists of Amsterdam and the icy Berlin winters to the sunny Mediterranean. But none of these great trains could rival the prestige of the Train Bleu, the epitome of cosseted chic, echoing in the blue of its name the azure of the hallowed coastline whose glittering popularity it shared.

Yet before the nineteenth century no one could have predicted that a string of obscure fishing villages, strung out along the Mediterranean coast from Marseille to Menton, would become the most select and sought-after of watering places for personages of means and fashion. It was the British who first "discovered" the Mediterranean coast, falling under the spell of its natural beauties and its balmy winters. Before long, London's wealthy and fashionable habitually forsook its winter fogs for the mimosa-scented breezes of the Riviera. Lord Brougham and Vaux, formerly Lord High Chancellor, was a pioneer in the field, settling in Cannes in the 1840s. The cream of the British aristocracy lost no time in following in his footsteps, with the blessing of Queen Victoria, who herself spent several winters in Nice and Cimiez at the Excelsior Hôtel Regina, which had been built with her needs in mind.

Now the elite from all over Europe wanted its share of winter sun, and rail services to the Riviera multiplied. Ever anxious to improve the conditions they could offer to their passengers, railway companies revised their itineraries and increased the complexity of their networks. Thus in 1889 the Calais–Nice–Rome Express, launched only six years earlier as the first train to connect England directly with Italy, via the Riviera, split in two to become the Calais–Rome Express and the Calais–Mediterranean Express. The former, passing through the famous Mont Cenis Tunnel, was to become the celebrated Rome Express. The latter was to be immortalized as the "Train Bleu."

In 1922, the Calais–Mediterranean Express did indeed become blue, as its varnished teak carriages were replaced by new steel ones, blue-liveried with gold lining. From the inauguration of this new look the train became known as the "Train Bleu." Replacing the old wooden carriages with steel ones brought with it huge advantages. Not only were they safer but they were also more comfortable, offering innovations such as single compartments for lone passengers—though in anticipation of every eventuality, including unexpected encounters, these compartments were furnished with communicating doors. Add to all this the smooth suspension, with each carriage mounted on forty springs, the electric lighting, and the mahogany-paneled corridors, and it is not difficult to see why this handsome blue with gold lining should have become synonymous with luxury. So indelible was the connection that the Compagnie Internationale des Wagons-Lits immediately set about repainting its entire rolling stock in blue.

The new train immediately inspired a devoted following, even across the Atlantic, as modish young ladies took to reserving their out of the pages of Scott Fitzgerald seats on the Train Bleu on board the steamer that brought them to France. There was one drawback, however: the

train was in service only from November to May. By the dawn of the Jazz Age this was a restriction that was out of step with the times, as chic travelers were no longer content merely to winter on the Riviera; now the summer months became all the rage too. In 1929, accordingly, the Train Bleu was refitted. The lacquer and shagreen decorations were given a fresh new look, while small fans placed at the head of the berths anticipated the summer heat. In a major innovation, the famous express to the Riviera now ran all year round, offering a daily service in both directions. In recognition of the continuing importance of its English clientele, a connecting train departed daily from Victoria Station in London, arriving at Folkestone in time for the midday ferry. After a Channel crossing that varied in length according to the sea conditions, the ferry would reach Calais in the early afternoon, where the Train Bleu would be waiting at the platform, polished and gleaming. Some three hours later it would reach the Gare du Nord in Paris, whence it would shunt backwards round Paris to the Gare du Lyon, where passengers starting their journey from Paris would join the train.

It was the golden rule that the train always left at seven-thirty sharp. It allowed the passengers enough time to find their compartment, settle in and dress for dinner, all before the bell for first service rang down the corridors. In the dining car, illumined by the warm light filtered by little lampshades in pink silk, dinner was served as the train rattled at full throttle through Fontainebleau and Sens, working up steam to haul the train's enormous weight (luxury trains weighed some 600 tons in the 1930s) up the exceedingly steep gradient into Burgundy. On this run, the fireman had to shovel coal into the firebox at a rate of one shovelful every two or three seconds. Other challenging features of the line included the Carnoules incline between Marseille and Ventimiglia, not to mention the effects of the Mistral, which when blowing at its strongest was reputed to be able to stop a train. Seven different locomotives, with seven different crews, took turns to haul the Train Bleu to its destination.

While all this was going on, the slumbering passengers continued their cosseted journey, arriving at Marseille at daybreak and crossing the Toulon viaduct as they breakfasted on scrambled eggs on toast. Here they were greeted by the spectacular sight of cascades of bougainvillea on either side of the tracks, with the rocks of the Esterel range flaming red in the sun. At eleven o'clock they arrived in Nice, and at twelve-thirty they reached the terminus at Ventimiglia.

From the 1950s, competition from air and road travel began to make itself felt. A temporary reprieve for the Train Bleu arrived in the form of the Cannes Film Festival, but the age of the TGV was approaching, sounding the death knell for the Train Bleu. Slowly, imperceptibly, standards dropped. In 1974, as a time-saving measure, the first service for dinner was served at the Gare de Lyon before departure. At around midnight the dining car was uncoupled, vanishing into the night and taking with it memories of breakfast at Toulon. Obscure schemes to improve profitability saw ordinary sleeping cars coupled to the Train Bleu, before gradually replacing the fabled blue carriages altogether. Then the saloon and dining cars suddenly vanished, to be replaced by an SNCF carriage which—adding insult to injury—boasted a livery in red. Stripped of its colors, the Train Bleu was set to enter the world of legend.

So here we are, heading for Nice. Farewell to the cold and foggy North! Here spring reigns supreme. The orange trees are weighed down with fruit; the olive trees, fig trees and date palms are in full flower; palms sway their plumes, and aloes scramble up the verges. The railway track is lined with rose hedges in bloom and fields of mignonettes and violets, which fill the air with their perfume. The line hugs the coast virtually all the way, running so close to the sea that the train sometimes seems to float on the blue waves. Sinuous as a snake, twisting and turning this way and that, the coastline unfolds in a succession of bays, headlands and coves, a fresh vista at every turn.

LUCIEN SOLVAY, 1882

192 ı The Train Bleu leaving for the Cannes Festival in 1959. At the carriage windows are prominent New Wave figures including Laurent Terzieff, Gérard Blain, Claude Chabrol, Roger Vadim and Annette Stroyberg.

205 ı Luggage label from the maiden journey of the Train Bleu in 1922. The London connection is mentioned, as is the short excursion into Italy via Ventimiglia and San Remo. Curiously, documents issued by the Wagons-Lits company were emblazoned with the name "Train Bleu" from the outset, although the name was not adopted officially until 1949.

206 ı The ceiling of the Train Bleu restaurant at the Gare de Lyon, Paris. The restaurant was built at the same time as the station (1895–1902), ready for the Exposition Universelle of 1900 and on behalf of the PLM (Paris–Lyon–Méditerranée) company. The painted panels framed by gilded moldings evoke the towns served by the company, a medley of sunlit landscapes, pinks and mimosa, and picturesque little harbours. The restaurant was extremely popular with British passengers, who viewed it as the first step on their journey to the Riviera. It was classified as a historic monument in 1972.

207 ı The bar on the Côte-d'Azur Pullman, the other luxury train owned by the Compagnie des Wagons-Lits that offered a daily service on the Paris–Ventimiglia

The first-class compartment was stifling; the vivid advertising cards of the railroad companies—The Pont du Gard at Arles, the Amphitheater at Orange, winter sports at Chamonix—were fresher than the long motionless sea outside. Unlike American trains that were absorbed in an intense destiny of their own, and scornful of people on another world less swift and breathless, this train was part of the country through which it passed. Its breath stirred the dust from the palm leaves, the cinders mingled with the dry dung in the gardens. Rosemary was sure she could lean from the window and pull flowers with her hand.

F. SCOTT FITZGERALD, 1933

208 ı An English advertisement for the new "Calais–Mediterranean Express," 1920s. One of the major line in the 1930s. On this train the bar, located in a corner of the dining car, appears to have functioned as a sort of gentlemen's club. It could never rival the prestige of the authentic Train Bleu bar, however, which was to open in 1951.

209 ı Two advertising posters for the Train Bleu. The right-hand

innovations of the Train Bleu was the single compartment, designed for lone travelers. The advertisement shows the berth in its day and night configurations, with all the advantages of electric lighting: each compartment was equipped with a blue night light and a bedside light.

210 ı Left: A mahogany-panelled corridor on the Train Bleu, 1922. In

poster, published by the Nord, PLM and Wagons-Lits companies, promotes the "new" Train Bleu, launched in 1929. That year the Train Bleu rolling stock was replaced, with the delivery of ninety sleeping cars with decorations by Maple, Morison, Nelson and René Prou.

211 ı A saloon car on the Côte d'Azur–Pullman Express, 1930s. these steel carriages, wood was reserved for purely decorative uses. Right: A decorative panel, made originally for the Côte d'Azur–Pullman Express. The design, of plane tree inlaid with bouquets of *pâte de verre* flowers, was created by the celebrated jeweler René Lalique in 1928.

Katherine wakened the next morning to brilliant sunshine. She went along to breakfast early ... When she returned to her compartment it had just been restored to its daytime appearance by the conductor, a dark man with a drooping moustache and melancholy face. ...

The man prepared to depart.

"We are rather late, Madame," he said. "I will let you know just before we get to Nice."

Katherine nodded. She sat by the window, entranced by the sunlit panorama. The palm trees, the deep blue of the sea, the bright yellow mimosa came with all the charm of novelty to the woman who for fourteen years had known only the drab winters of England.

AGATHA CHRISTIE, 1928

200

The atmosphere in these daytime services was very different from that of the night trains. At mealtimes, for instance, passengers on the Train Bleu would drift towards the dining car, while those on the Côte d'Azur–Pullman Express waited in their seats to be served. In this way, passengers on its maiden voyage negotiated their way through *pâté de canard périgourdine* and *selle de veau Orloff*, washed down with Meursault Goutte d'Or 1923 and Mumm Cordon Rouge champagne from the same year.

212 ı The Train Bleu bar, 1950s. In 1951, one of the handsome Lalique-decorated saloon cars of the Côte d'Azur–Pullman Express was incorporated into the Train Bleu, where one half of it was fitted out as a dining room and the other half as a bar. As chic and celebrated in its time as that of the Ritz, the Train Bleu bar was to remain a meeting place of choice for a wealthy cosmopolitan elite until 1976.

213 ı The Train Bleu *voiture-bar*, restored by the Compagnie des Wagons-Lits and now a historic monument. This carriage and seven others, all equally prestigious, now form the Pullman Orient Express, which offers a programme of events and charter trips to passengers nostalgic for the golden age of the great night sleepers.

214 ı René Lalique's *Bacchanalian Maidens* triptych, designed in the late 1920s for the

COMPAGNIE INTERNATIONALE
DES WAGONS-LITS

CALAIS-MÉDITERRANÉE
EXPRESS

Wagons-Lits 1re et 2e cl.   Sleeping-Cars 1st and 2nd cl.
(London) CALAIS-PARIS-NICE-VENTIMIGLIA

saloon cars of the Côte. d'Azur–Pullman Express and executed in Cuban mahogany and *pâte de verre*.

215 ı Train Bleu dining car, 1950s. These dining cars posed problems from the outset, as in order to give diners more room they seated only 42 passengers, as opposed to 52 or even 56 on other trains. This meant that dinner had to be served in two sittings, leading to complaints from the half of the passengers who were kept waiting. The solution to the problem was found in 1951 with the addition of the saloon car composed of a second dining room and the celebrated bar, where passengers could while away the time agreeably, glass in hand.

216 ı A lady passenger comfortably ensconced in the Côte d'Azur–Pullman Express, 1930s.

217 ı The monumental steps leading up to the Gare Saint-Charles, Marseille. Many Train Bleu passengers took advantage of a brief scheduled stop at Marseille (to reverse and change locomotives) to take breakfast there. Others preferred to sip their morning coffee a little later, as the train steamed over the viaduct at Toulon.

218 ı Left: Lady passengers taking tea in their compartment, 1930s. Right: Poster by Charles Hallo aimed at the British and American clientele who had launched the vogue for summer holidays on the Côte d'Azur; from

I did not visit Nice or Monte Carlo until I was over thirty. Yet my first experience of the Midi has left me with memories as potent as those of early childhood. ... At daybreak, just after Marseille I remember, the horizon was tinged with a particular shade of blue, dense, solid and clearly set off against the near-white of the sky. The new sail of a small boat overlapped it, sparkled and vanished. A sheet of flaming purple poured over yellow walls alongside the train as it slowed down, and a voice informed me of the name of this lava flow of flowers: "bougainvillea." Then, through stiff, glossy foliage unruffled by the wind, I saw a hundred lights in the shape of bulging spheres. The voice came again: "mandarins"; and at that moment a curtain of oleanders and mimosa covered everything, with the sun peeping through ...

COLETTE, 1932

1929 the Train Bleu, hitherto in service only from November to May, ran throughout the year.

219 | A Riviera landscape, c. 1895. After Marseille the line hugged the shoreline for a large part of the way, offering magnificent panoramas over the Mediterranean.

He walked up St James's Street, across Piccadilly, and strolled along in the direction of Piccadilly Circus. As he passed the offices of Messrs Thomas Cook & Sons [he] went in. The office was comparatively empty, and he got attended to at once.

"I want to go to Nice next week. Will you give me particulars?"

"What date, sir?"

"The fourteenth. What is the best train?"

"Well, of course, the best train is what they call 'The Blue Train.' You avoid the tiresome Customs business at Calais."

Derek nodded. He knew all this, none better.

"The fourteenth," murmured the clerk; "that is rather soon. The Blue Train is nearly always booked up."

"See if there is a berth left," said Derek. "If there is not –" He left the sentence unfinished, with a curious smile on his face.

The clerk disappeared for a few minutes, and presently returned. "That is all right, sir; still three berths left. I will book you one of them. What name?" ...

The clerk nodded … and turned his attention to the next client.

"I want to go to Nice—on the fourteenth. Isn't there a train called the Blue Train?"

Agatha Christie, 1928

COMPAGNIE INTERNATIONALE

DES

WAGONS-LITS

ET DES

GRANDS EXPRESS EUROPÉENS

TRAIN-BLEU

(LONDON)-CALAIS-PARIS-MARSEILLE

NICE - VENTIMIGLIA

SAN-REMO

The Sleeping Car & International Express Trains Company

The New Single-Berth Sleeping Cars of the Train-de-Luxe (Calais-Mediterranean Express)

AT NIGHT

BY DAY

COMPAGNIE INTERNATIONALE DES WAGONS-LITS ET DES GRANDS EXPRESS EUROPÉENS

LE NOUVEAU TRAIN BLEU VERS LA COTE D'AZUR

217

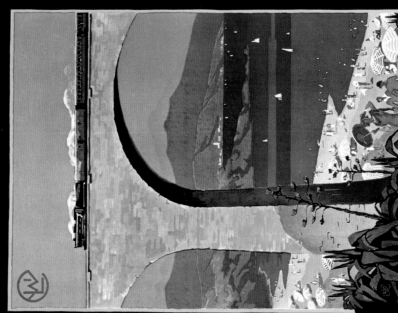

SUMMER ON THE FRENCH RIVIERA
BY THE BLUE TRAIN

1923

THE BLUE TRAIN

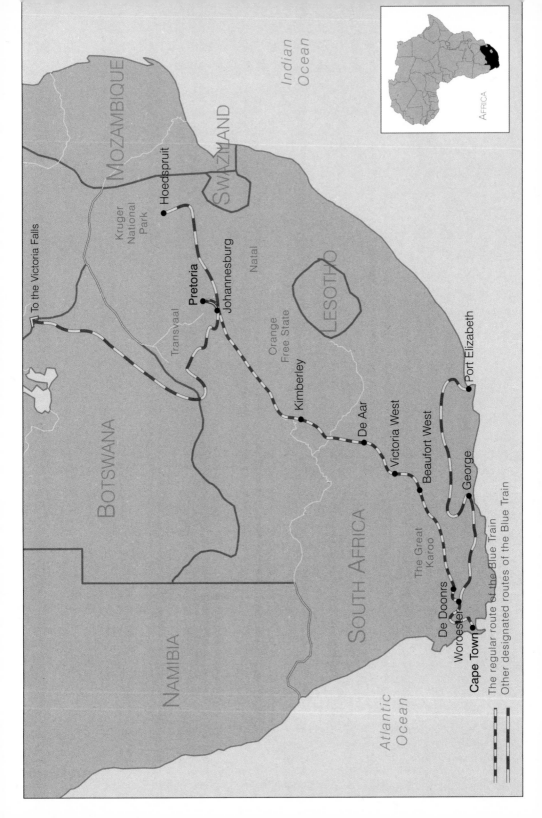

AFRICA

Indian
Ocean

MOZAMBIQUE

SWAZILAND

Hoedspruit

Kruger
National
Park

To the Victoria Falls

Pretoria

Johannesburg

Transvaal

Natal

LESOTHO

Orange
Free State

BOTSWANA

Kimberley

De Aar

Victoria West

Port Elizabeth

Beaufort West

NAMIBIA

SOUTH AFRICA

George

The Great
Karoo

De Doorns

Worcester

Cape Town

Atlantic
Ocean

The regular route of the Blue Train
Other designated routes of the Blue Train

Launched within a year of the Train Bleu, the Blue Train also shared the same color, the same pedigree—the lineage of luxury express trains—and even, curiously, the same habit of going under two different names at once. Officially named the "Union Limited" or "Union Express," the southern African train has always been known simply as the Blue Train. But there the similarities end. While the Train Bleu transported the gilded elite of the northern hemisphere to the sunlit playgrounds of the Riviera, the Blue Train conjured up dreams in the southern hemisphere of what it might have been: a great trans-African line running from the Cape to Cairo.

The earliest railway in southern Africa was launched on the east coast on 26 June 1860 by the Natal Railway Company, running barely three kilometers (two miles) from Point into Durban and initially drawn by oxen. By 1862 the Cape Town Railway, begun in 1859 but held up by administrative delays and the mountainous granite terrain, had progressed by a mere 34 kilometers. At this period the Cape Colony was still sparsely populated by settlers and had virtually no industries, exporting only wool, ivory and leather. Its roads were inferior, and it had no banks. Britain was the dominant power, but viewed the colony as a paltry and insignificant corner of the mighty empire "on which the sun never set." But all this was soon to change. In 1867, to the north of the Orange River, the first diamond was found. Prospectors stampeded to make their fortunes, and the British—suddenly galvanized into action—started negotiations over ownership of the diamond fields with the Boer Republics founded by early Dutch settlers. While this was going on, the immense diamond field of Kimberley was discovered, triggering the world's greatest diamond rush. By the end of the century a prosperous settlement had grown up there, and South Africa had been catapulted into the modern industrial world. Now work began in earnest on a rail network, further prompted by the discovery of gold deposits on the border between the Transvaal and Bechuanaland.

Cecil Rhodes, prominent British-born businessman and prime minister of the Cape Colony from 1890 to 1896, now pulled off a spectacular coup. Through a series of financial deals that were as shrewd as they were ambitious he managed to secure the world monopoly on the mining and selling of South African diamonds for his company, De Beers. And what he could achieve for himself he could also achieve for the British Empire: in the name of the British Crown, he left no stone unturned in his—ultimately successful—attempts to deprive the Boers of their ownership of the Transvaal gold mines. His great dream and obsession, however, was the building of a railway that would run the length of Africa without ever leaving British territory, "from the Cape to Cairo."

The first step of this grandiose plan was the opening of the great South African line running from Cape Town to the Kimberley mines, and then continuing on to Johannesburg where, in 1886, a small-scale prospector by the name of George Harrison had stumbled upon an outcrop of rock seamed with gold. Three years later Johannesburg had expanded to become the largest city in South Africa. The line continued onwards, in 1905 reaching the spectacular Victoria Falls, where the Zambezi River plunges down a chasm 108 meters (360 feet) deep and 1.7 kilometers (1 mile) wide. The railway line begun in Cairo in 1856 reached Khartoum in the 1890s; other branches of the line penetrated further south, as far as Wau in the Sudan. From Cape Town the line ran north as far as Uganda. But between Uganda and the Sudan there was nothing. Though the idea has never been completely abandoned, the Cape-to-Cairo railway was to remain unfinished.

In 1923 the young Union of South Africa—formed in 1910 by the federation of the provinces of the Cape, Natal, Transvaal and Orange Free State—launched its first major express train, known as the "Union Limited" on its northbound journey and the "Union Express" on the southbound return. In Cape Town it met the ocean liners that steamed into harbor seventeen days after leaving Southampton, before heading north-east to the gold fields of Johannesburg and Pretoria. The pride of the new nation, it was fitted out in sumptuous style from 1927. Ten years later, it exchanged its wooden carriages for steel ones built in Birmingham, equipped with air conditioning and painted blue. Henceforth it was known as the Blue Train, although the name did not receive official sanction until 1946. In 1972 new carriages replaced the old ones, and in 1997 it was completely and comprehensively refurbished and redesigned, right down to the smallest rivet.

This is the train that now, several times a month, invites passengers to relive the dream of Cecil Rhodes, from Cape Town to Pretoria and back. The (substantial) price of the tickets includes everything on board—with the exception, as the manager explains to new arrivals, of "caviar, French champagne and external telephone calls." Here you leave reality behind when you board. This is no ordinary train, but rather something between a limousine, a fairytale coach and a flying carpet. To the discerning traveler the Blue Train offers marble-lined bathrooms, suites with bathtubs, three temperatures of water in the taps (hot, cold and iced), individually regulated air conditioning in each suite, and—the supreme luxury—a leisurely pace at which to indulge in it all, the train's maximum speed being fixed at 90 kph (58 mph).

On the journey from Cape Town to Pretoria, the train passes through tree-lined suburbs and the windswept sands of the Cape Flats before reaching the vineyards (scarlet in autumn) of the Paarl region and the Hex Valley, dotted here and there with small farms marked by white porticoes and cypress trees. The outside world unfolds beyond the smoked glass of the windows, unless passengers prefer to repair to the club car, where they can watch the driver's-eye view of the surrounding country shot from the front of the train and projected live on to a giant screen.

Just before nightfall the train crosses the parched desert of the Karoo, and then it is time to dress for dinner (the dress code is formal), followed, perhaps, by a nightcap in the bar as the Southern Cross blazes in the starry night sky. In the morning the sun rises over the maize fields of

the Transvaal, with spoil heaps in shades of yellow and brown signaling the presence of a string of gold-mining towns. Then in the distance the white sunlight flashes off the glass and steel office blocks of Johannesburg. Soon the train will reach the end of its journey at Pretoria, one day, two hours and forty-five minutes after leaving Cape Town.

Johannesburg Station in 1914.

On leaving Cape Town, the train passes first of all through the midst of flourishing farms. These are small white houses, very pleasant in appearance, shaded by old trees and surrounded by fields and well-cultivated vines, for this is above all a wine-growing region. But after a few miles the country becomes wilder, and soon the valley of the Hex River opens up. The train runs between high mountains covered with stunted vegetation, climbs up onto the immense plateau that forms a large part of South Africa, and crosses the Karoo desert; not a sandy desert like the ones we drew at school, but a vast undulating expanse, with scattered patches of sparse greenery. Meager as it was, this terrain seemed to suit the ostriches; we encountered some looking for food, and they regarded the train with a casual air as it passed before them.

ETHEL M. BAGG, 1913

220 | The Blue Train, pride of the young Union of South Africa, in 1946. To protect patriotic sensibilities, its name is inscribed on the front of the engine in both English and Afrikaans ("Bloutrein"), the two official languages at that time.

229 | The Blue Train leaving Cape Town. In the background is the characteristic outline of Table Mountain, the monolithic slab of granite that dominates the bay.

230 | This station between Cape Town and Kimberley, photographed in verascope by Lowrdon in 1902, does not yet have a name, only a number.

231 | Left: The steward, known grandly on the Blue Train as the butler, greets passengers on the platform and delivers them to their suites. Right: A corner of the club car, the only carriage with a smoking area.

232-233 | Cabin service with, from left to right, a bathroom with shower; a butler preparing the suite for the night; and toiletries bearing the Blue Train monogram. Luxury suites with twin beds have a bath, while De Luxe suites with twin beds have a shower, and those with a double bed have a bath.

234 | A luxury suite laid out for the night. Space was the overriding problem in the design of the train's internal arrangements. The standard width for passenger cars on South African railways, 2.85m, has here been widened to an exceptional 2.9m, thus gaining a whole

226

Wherever the train stops to take on water ... natives crowd around in the most picturesque costumes and attitudes. ...All the country through which we pass is fairly monotonous, but the reflections of the light change in such a marvelous fashion that one does not tire of it. Nevertheless, I am sure that all the passengers will be exceedingly happy to arrive at Bulawayo, or to devote just a few hours to making the excursion to the Matoppos, where the tomb of Cecil Rhodes lies. This is what we decide to do. But many prefer to stay in the very comfortable hotel at Bulawayo, from where one can visit the ruins of Gwelo and the district of Zimbabwe. The railway does not yet reach the Matoppos, but the line will soon be finished.

ETHEL M. BAGG, 1913

50mm. A few more millimeters were saved by shaving down the thickness of the side walls, so bringing an overall gain in internal width of 88mm.

235 | The Blue Train crossing a wooded ravine in the Eastern Cape, on a secondary line serving the east coast and known as the "Garden Route" (not on the normal route). Other—more

affordable—trains also run on this extremely popular route: the steam-hauled Outeniqua Choo-Tjoe between George and Knysna, for example, is beloved of steam aficionados.

236 | Left: A luxury suite in its daytime configuration. Right: Passengers may tuck into their full English breakfast either in their suites or in the dining car.

237 | The dining room seats 42 passengers. Calls for the two luncheon and dinner services are given on a xylophone and in three languages.

238-239 | The menu features local specialities such as Karoo Desert carré of lamb and Oudtshoorn ostrich steak, washed down—naturally—with fine wines from the Paarl vineyards, the

Franschhoek Valley (famed for its white wines) and the Constantia Valley, whose wines are aged in Cape cellars. French Huguenot vignerons imported their expertise and experience to this "new world" in the seventeenth century, and nowadays wine-lovers are spoilt for choice.

240-241 | Two views of the club car, a crowded spot in the

[At Bulawayo] you climb back into the train for the short journey that remains to reach the Zambezi. The country has changed completely in appearance. Everywhere are giant trees, forming an entire forest, with the smooth multiple trunks of baobabs here and there. This is a country of lions, giraffe and several species of antelope; but the wild animals do not deign to come and inspect our train, and we do not glimpse their shadows. Yet at one station the driver showed us the skeleton of an elephant which, the year before, had rashly fallen asleep on the rails and had caused the train twelve or thirteen hours' delay.

ETHEL M. BAGG, 1913

evenings. Afternoon tea is served daily in the separate lounge car.
242 ı One of the train sets has a conference car equipped with all the latest audio-visual equipment for presentations. When it is not in use for business meetings, its large windows make it an ideal observation car.
243 ı The great railway bridge over the Zambezi, first

constructed in 1905, with the Victoria Falls behind. Departing from Pretoria, the Blue Train makes this spectacular trip through Botswana and Zimbabwe on an occasional basis.

THE CALIFORNIA ZEPHYR

1949

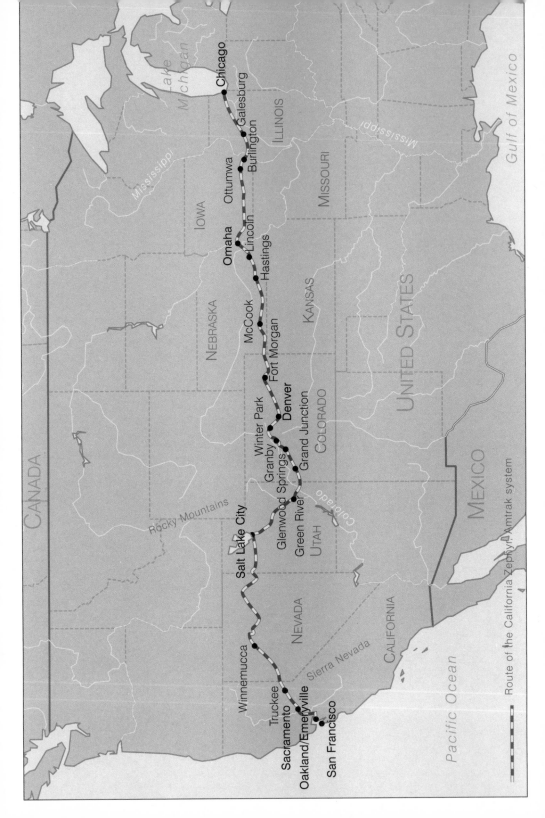

Route of the California Zephyr Amtrak system

At about noon on 10 May 1869, at a remote spot called Promontory Summit, "a desert without water or shade" in Utah, one of the most celebrated episodes in the history of railways reached its climax, as the last sleeper was put in place and the last spike driven on the first transcontinental railway to cross America. Seated at a table beside the track, a telegraph operator waited, his finger poised, ready to transmit. In Omaha and in Chicago to the east, other operators waited to transmit his message on to the President and to every town in the United States. Back at Promontory Summit, the crowd that had gathered blocked the telegraph operator's view of the track, but their thunderous applause told him that the deed was accomplished: the last spike (gold-plated for the occasion) had been driven. The message that raced down the wires, laconic though it was, was to be the cause of rejoicing throughout America: "Done."

Seven years earlier, President Abraham Lincoln signed the federal law of 1 July 1862 authorizing two railroad companies to build a transcontinental line: the Union Pacific would start from Omaha in the east, while the Central Pacific would take Sacramento in the west as its starting point. Initially work was slow and fraught with difficulties. By 1864, as the Civil War swallowed up men and equipment, the

Union Pacific had only progressed by a few kilometers. On the Central Pacific side, meanwhile, construction work had come up against the obstacle of the Sierra Nevada. Only 55 kilometers out of Sacramento, explosives were already being used.

After the Civil War had ended, matters improved for the railway. Between 1867 and 1869 progress of work across the deserts of Utah and Nevada could justly be described as stupendous: in just two years 2800 kilometers of track were laid, as compared with the decade that it took to build the line from Paris to Marseille. True, the work was not exactly meticulous in its attention to detail, but America was in a hurry. As the Central Pacific and Union Pacific locomotives came cow-catcher to cow-catcher at Promontory Summit, it was time for the whole nation to shift into a higher gear. No more perilous six-month odysseys in covered wagons to cross the continent. No more long-winded detours via Cape Horn or the malarial swamps of Panama. If you wanted to travel from the Atlantic to the Pacific, if you wanted to join the gold rush in Colorado or stake a land claim in the Wild West, now all you had to do was buy a train ticket. Ambushes and acts of sabotage, hold-ups by outlaws and native Americans, snowdrifts on the line and trestle bridges collapsing into ravines: all this would now become part of the mythology of the American West. Although there have been no trains at Promontory Summit since 1903, the visitor centre at the Golden Spike National Historic Site there is now home to steam locomotives Jupiter and 119, fully functional replicas of the original locomotives which carry out a daily re-enactment of the "Wedding of the Rails" ceremony of 10 May 1869. The train that still largely follows the route taken by the pioneers of the American West is the California Zephyr, affectionately known as the CZ, now run by Amtrak. From Chicago to Emeryville (for San Francisco), the CZ offers two and a half days of luxury travel and breathtaking views.

In 1934 the Burlington company launched the prototype "Zephyr," and the first run of this new "streamliner," from Denver to Chicago, caused a sensation. The first American streamlined diesel-powered train, it boasted a sleek, gleaming allure, all stainless steel and cutting-edge glamour. But the Zephyr was not just a tour-de-force of industrial design and engineering. Anticipating the needs of a new type of clientele, including families, it offered a whole new concept in train travel. In 1936 the Burlington introduced its "Zephyrettes," hand-picked, educated young women—

part hostess, part nanny, part tour guide and part nurse—resplendent in their two-piece suits and military-style hats, whose responsibility it was to tend to passengers' needs while on board. Another stroke of genius on the Burlington's part was the later introduction of the "Vista Dome," a glazed, raised dome that offered passengers spectacular all-round views and that was to become the hallmark of the Zephyr fleet. "Look up, look down, look all around… ride the Vista Dome," urged an advertisement from the 1940s.

Another forerunner of the California Zephyr was the Exposition Flyer, which ran from Chicago to Oakland under the joint management of the three major western railroad companies: the Burlington Route from Chicago to Denver, the Denver & Rio Grande Western Railroad from Denver to Salt Lake City, and finally the Western Pacific from Salt Lake City to Oakland. Like the Zephyr fleet, the Flyer placed great emphasis on the warmth of the welcome and standards of comfort it offered, with Pullman cars, air conditioning in all classes and fine dining, and on the beauty of the landscapes through which it passed. Enshrining the slogan "The Scenic way Across America," it was an instant success: although originally intended only to serve the

San Francisco Golden Gate Exposition of 1939, it remained in service until 1949.

This was the year in which the same three companies decided to launch the California Zephyr. With is sleek silver livery, its charming Zephyrettes, its five Vista Domes per train and a panoply of practical innovations such as showers in the cabins, the "Silver Lady," as it became known, lived up to its slogan of being "The Most Talked-About Train in America." Even the timetable was carefully thought through in both directions, ensuring that the train crossed the monotonous expanses of the plains and deserts of Nevada during the night, so that at daybreak the Rockies or the Feather River Canyon would be revealed in all their splendor. On its first run, from Oakland to Chicago, lady passengers were presented with specially imported Hawaiian orchids in the CZ colors of silver and orange, and the Western Pacific band played the train out of Oakland Station. Already the Silver Lady was the stuff of legend, living up effortlessly to its own publicity: "The new California Zephyr brings exciting innovations to train travel. This transcontinental luxury train—Diesel-powered, streamlined and built of gleaming stainless steel—provides new thrills and new pleasure to the fortunate travelers who ride it."

The California Zephyr was to remain in service for twenty years and two days before succumbing to the inevitable competition from road and air travel. The Denver & Rio Grande Western Railroad took up the baton with the Rio Grande Zephyr, which for twelve years served the Denver–Salt Lake City line with considerable flair and equally considerable difficulties. In 1983 Amtrak re-introduced the CZ, with revised and updated trains from which devoted aficionados of the old CZ—and there are many—have yet to recover. On the Amtrak trains the handsome Vista Domes have given way to comfortable two-tier ("bi-level") Superliner passenger cars, while in the diner the excellent and freshly prepared local trout of yesteryear have yielded to deep-frozen hamburgers. Yet some of the breathless excitement of the journey on the Silver Lady in her 1950s heyday lives on: "Magnificent mountain vistas you can really see! Snow-capped splendors in the colorful Colorado Rockies and California's Feather River Canyon during daylight hours. The most *enjoyable* ride between Chicago and California!"

So now we shall cross the distance that separates us from the East in a single journey, stopping only at Chicago and Niagara Falls. To do this we shall take the central route, the first established by the three great railway companies, who will manage it jointly. The southern line, opened a few years ago, goes south as far as the frontier with Mexico, passing via Santa Fe, the oldest town in the New World, and Kansas City, one of the most rapidly developing centers in the United States. The northern line, running close to the Canadian border, will run to the famous Yellowstone Park, a recently discovered marvel.

HUGUES KRAFFT, 1885

244 ⏐ The Amtrak California Zephyr in Chicago Union Station, 1985. On American railways "coach" class is traditionally the most economic way to travel, with extra comforts limited to reclining seats.

257 ⏐ The "Wedding of the Rails": the meeting of the Central Pacific and Union Pacific tracks at Promontory Summit, 10 May 1869. This photograph by Charles Savage shows the two locomotives, the Union Pacific 119 and the Central Pacific Jupiter, coming cow-catcher to cow-catcher, amid a crowd of engineers and labourers, both American and Chinese.

258 ⏐ Departure of the California Limited, a Californian coastal service, c.1900. When Abraham Lincoln launched the transcontinental railway project in 1862, at the beginning of the American Civil War, he hoped that it might help to persuade the wealthy and flourishing state of California not to secede from the Union. The gambit worked.

259 ⏐ The magnificent Beaux-Arts style Chicago Union Station, designed in white and pink marble by Daniel Burnham (dictum: "make no small plans, they have no magic to stir men's blood"). The station served four railway companies: the Pennsylvania; the Chicago, Burlington & Quincy; the Chicago, Milwaukee & St Paul; and the Chicago & Alton.

260 ⏐ Union Pacific locomotive 25, 1880s. Immortalized in

The light of the sinking sun glorified the Sierras, and as the dew fell, aromatic odors made the still air sweet. On a single track, at times coursing along a narrow ledge carved from the mountain side by men lowered from the top in baskets, overhanging ravines from 2,000 to 3,000 feet deep, the monster train snaked its way upwards, stopping sometimes in front of a few frame houses, at others where nothing was to be seen but a log cabin with a few Chinamen hanging about it, but where trails on the sides of the ravines pointed to a gold country above and below.

ISABELLA L. BIRD, 1888

Westerns, American locomotives were immediately recognizable by their tenders laden with wood or coal, their bogies (also a feature of every other carriage) to ensure a smoother ride on hastily laid tracks, their lofty engineers' cabs, their enormous headlights, and of course their famous cow-catchers.

261 ǀ A typical American passenger car, with a central aisle flanked by seats, and foldaway bunks above, photochrome, c.1900. The length of journeys undertaken in America dictated a degree of comfort earlier than in Europe.

262 ǀ Burlington Zephyr 9900 is christened with champagne, Philadelphia, 18 April 1934.

263 ǀ Above left: Postcard showing the California Zephyr in the Rockies, 1950s. The CZ railroad companies produced their own postcards for the use of their passengers, which it was part of the Zephyrettes' job to mail at the next stop. Above right: A CZ observation dome, 1950s. Below left: A CZ dining car, originally designed to accommodate 48 diners, 1949.

264 ǀ Left: A California Zephyr chef awaits supplies in Denver Union Station, 1985. Right: Luncheon menu from the dining car of the Exposition Flyer, February 1943. The suggested

Below right: The CZ in the station at Galesburg, Illinois, a postcard published by the Illinois Camera Shop, 1950s. Inset: A Zephyr luggage label.

Here is the famous Golden Gate, the narrow strait through which we will reach the great bay of San Francisco. The coastline is rocky yet covered with grass; to our right stretches the young capital of California, a grayish mass of houses strung out over the hills; to our left, in the distance, appear the houses of Oakland on the far bank. That is where we board the train that will carry us across the New World.

HUGUES KRAFFT, 1885

252

entrées had a pronounced local flavor, including "Yankee Pot Roast with Rice" and "Omelette, Western style," accompanied (intriguingly) by "Hot Ginger Bread" and followed by "Jell-O" or "Cherry Cobbler." Fresh fish was always available, and until 1983 trout was the Zephyr's gastronomic speciality.

265 ı Dining car kitchen on the California Zephyr, 1985. Gastronomy has been superseded by efficiency: dishes are no longer prepared in the kitchen, as on the old Zephyrs, but are brought on board ready-prepared.

266 ı Bison grazing along the route of the California Zephyr, 1985. The virtual extinction of the bison, with catastrophic effects for the native Americans who depended upon it for food and much else, was partly the result of the building of the railway. The wholesale slaughter of millions of animals by the settlers was only exacerbated by the need to feed the huge army of laborers who worked on the railway.

267 ı Dining car attendants on the California Zephyr prepare for the next sitting, 1985.

268 ı The westbound California Zephyr near Kremmling, some 160km north-west of Denver, October 2002.

269 ı Crossing the Rockies by Tennessee Pass, between Colorado Springs and Denver, verascope, c.1900. The Denver & Rio Grande Railroad, responsible for the transcontinental railway

One day soon after I was born, one of our scouts returned to the camp in a state of high excitement, saying that he had seen a great snake slithering across the prairie. This caused a great sensation. Careful observation revealed a plume of smoke following what he had taken to be a snake. It was the first train of the Union Pacific Railroad. For the Indians this was very curious, and they started to climb up to vantage points from which they could watch the train move and hear the strange noises that it made. When they saw that the "snake" slithered along a metal track from which it did not stray, they grew bolder, and drew nearer to examine it more closely.

CHIEF STANDING BEAR OF THE OGLALA SIOUX,
LAST QUARTER OF THE 19TH CENTURY

Detail from an advertisement showing a Santa Fe locomotive, 1948.

between Denver and Salt Lake City, was renowned for its skill at crossing high mountains. The track that it laid via Tennessee Pass in 1887, reaching an altitude of 3121m (10,240ft), remains to this day the highest in the United States.

270 | The Rockies viewed from the observation car of the California Zephy, 1985.

271 | After the immense plains of the Mississippi, the California Zephyr embarks on its thrilling crossing of the Rockies, 1985. In preparation for this challenging leg of the journey, it stops at Denver to change locomotives.

272-273 | Panoramic view of Marshall Pass, Colorado, photographed by William Henry Jackson in photochrome, 1880s.

The construction of the Marshall Pass route in 1880 was a heroic episode in the history of the railway in Colorado. The gradient on both sides was so steep that the trains were generally hauled by several locomotives, and after the first snows the pass became even harder to negotiate, necessitating constant snow clearance. From the late 1880s

253

Far left: The
Burlington Zephyr in
1936.
Left: Zephyrette in a
Vista Dome.

254

transcontinental traffic was rerouted via Tennessee Pass. The legendary Marshall Pass route went into slow decline, until at last it was abandoned in the 1950s.

274-275 ꞁ The eastbound California Zephyr between Green River, Utah, and Grand Junction, Colorado, 1990s.

276 ꞁ Left: Landing stage on the lake at Salt Lake City, c.1900.

During the construction of the transcontinental railway, Brigham Young – first governor of Utah territory and president of the Church of Jesus Christ of the Latter-day Saints, known as the Mormons—wanted the new line to run through Salt Lake City. For technical and financial reasons, however, the Central Pacific and Union Pacific companies decided

to follow a more northerly route, via Promontory Summit. From January 1870 Salt Lake City was connected to the new line, however, and soon it became known as the "crossroads of the West."

Right: "Milepost Map" of the Western Pacific section of the Exposition Flyer route, 1939.

278 ꞁ View from the observation car of the California Zephyr, 1985. All the seats face outwards, and to help passengers decide which side will have the most spectacular view, Amtrak supplies a map showing all the best viewpoints, with a little camera symbol everywhere where passengers might want to have their cameras ready.

279 ꞁ The Ferry Building, San

Precisely at 11 in the evening, the huge Pacific train, with its heavy bell tolling, thundered up to the door of the Truckee House, and on presenting my ticket at the double door of a "Silver Palace" car, the slippered steward, whispering low, conducted me to my berth—a luxurious bed three and a half feet wide, with a hair mattress on springs, fine linen sheets, and costly California blankets. The twenty-four inmates of the car were all invisible, asleep behind rich curtains. It was a true Temple of Morpheus. Profound sleep was the object to which everything was dedicated. Four silver lamps hanging from the roof, and burning low, gave a dreamy light. On each side of the center passage, rich rep curtains, green and crimson, striped with gold, hung from silver bars running near the roof, and trailed on the soft Axminster carpet. The temperature was carefully kept at 70 degrees. It was 29 degrees outside. Silence and freedom from jolting were secured by double doors and windows, costly and ingenious arrangements of springs and cushions, and a speed limited to eighteen miles an hour.

ISABELLA L. BIRD, 1888

Francisco, verascope, 1909.
No Zephyr ever in fact ran to San Francisco: the California Zephyr made only a brief appearance in the city for its official inauguration on 19 March 1949. The Zephyrs' western terminus was always Oakland, and now Emeryville. There passengers would disembark in order to cross the bay—originally by ferry, now by bus or taxi over the Bay Bridge—to reach San Francisco, their final destination on the far shore.

THE
CALIFORNIA
LIMITED
LOS ANGELES
SAN DIEGO.
SAN FRANCISCO.

Santa Fe

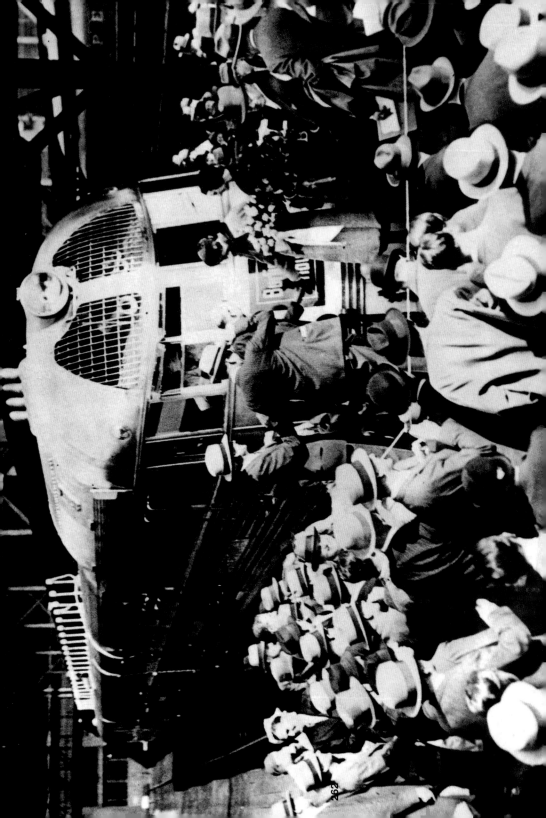

California Zephyr—Burlington Rou
Galesburg, Illinois

263

Exposition Flyer

MENU

SAN FRANCISCO'S CABLE CARS

Dining Car

264

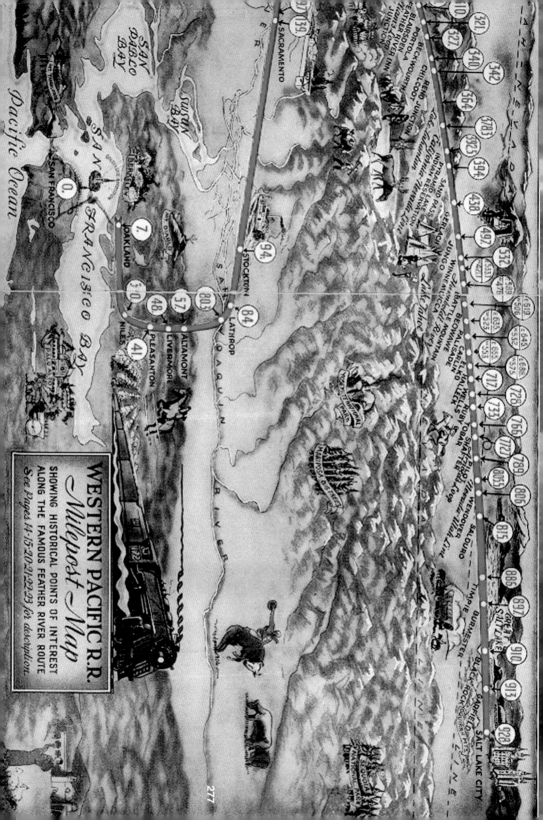

WESTERN PACIFIC R.R.
~Milepost~Map

SHOWING HISTORICAL POINTS OF INTEREST
ALONG THE FAMOUS FEATHER RIVER ROUTE

See Pages 14-15-20-21-22-23 for description.

277

LOUNGE CAR

1981

THE PALACE ON WHEELS

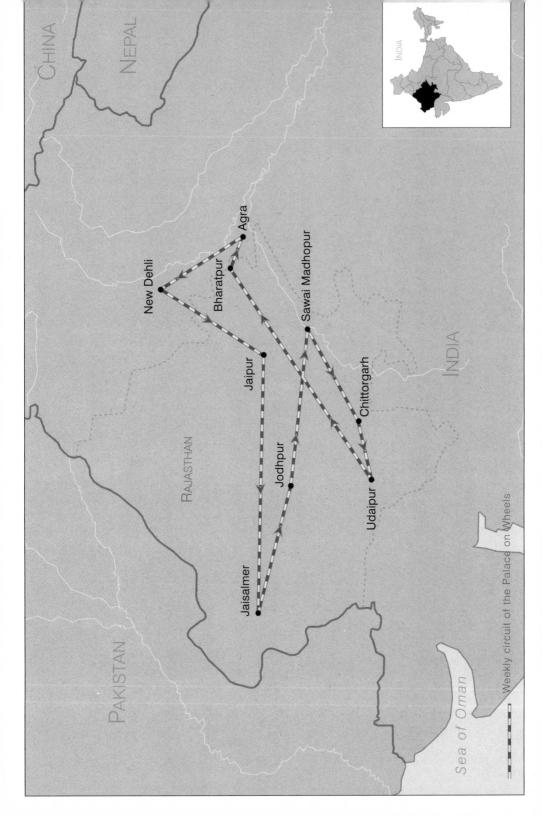

Weekly circuit of the Palace on Wheels

From the moment when the inaugural train on the first section of the Great Indian Peninsula Railway steamed out of Bori Bunder station Bombay (now Mumbai) on 16 April 1853, to the accompaniment of a twenty-one gun salute, the history of India and of its railways became inextricably intertwined. Combining British engineering flair with Indian ingenuity, the railways of the Subcontinent—or their superior accommodation at least—rivaled the finest trains in the world, in the comforts they offered. The French academician and ardent anglophile André Chevrillon, traveling in northwestern India in the 1880s, was enchanted: "I greatly admire the Indian railways. The carriages are furnished with bathrooms in which one can take a shower, with couchettes to let down when one wants to stretch out, and to which all travelers in first and second class are entitled at night ... Thus we traverse a distance of two thousand kilometers without fatigue, all the while pitying the poor souls who, having left Paris on an evening train, arrive at Marseille or Brest worn out and feverish from lack of sleep." If sahib was hungry, he had only to alert a passing attendant. There was always the heat, of course, by which many western travelers were utterly prostrated. But here too their needs were anticipated, as stations put spacious bathrooms at their disposal, in which they could luxuriate in a cool bath before receiving the ministrations of a professional masseur. And if the connection was a leisurely one, sleeping accommodation could even be provided, with female employees in attendance.

However sybaritic and luxurious these arrangements might have been, however, they were as nothing compared with the fabulous trains that many Indian princes built for their own enjoyment, to impress their subjects and to astonish their colonial masters. Many Indian princes were handsomely rewarded for their loyalty to the British, who in return for their allegiance to the crown guaranteed the continuance of the princes' staggering privileges and maintained the (hugely unequal) social order. Under the Raj, local potentates sometimes indulged in wild and idiosyncratic excesses. In the years before independence, Maharajah Kishan Singh of Bharatpur bought no fewer than twenty-two Rolls-Royces. A Maharajah of Jodhpur built an airport and acquired a flotilla of aircraft. Those who hankered after their own railway, meanwhile, were often given government assistance in building them when it suited the strategic or economic needs of the Raj. Thus princes of fabulous wealth, such as the Nizam of Hyderabad and the Gaekwar of Baroda, either traveled in their own luxuriously appointed trains or received special permission to couple their own carriages—complete with throne rooms and zenanas for Hindu ladies in purdah—to scheduled train services.

With the decline of the British Empire, leading to India's independence in 1947, the princes of India found their wealthy lifestyles curtailed, but it was Prime Minister Indira Gandhi who finally abolished their royal titles, privy purses and privileges in 1971. Royal palaces were now turned into luxury hotels, and Indian Railways decided to pension off the magnificent royal railway coaches, which languished in depots and sidings for the next ten years.

It was in 1981–82 that the Rajasthan Tourism Development Corporation, working with Indian Railways, decided to rescue twenty royal carriages, and on 26 January 1982 the sumptuous steam-hauled Palace on Wheels made its inaugural journey, instantly becoming the most prestigious train on the Subcontinent. Those who were fortunate enough to travel on the train before its refurbishment in the late 1980s were given an unforgettable taste of the elegance and decadence of the Raj, in authentic carriages dating back—in the case of the

carriage that once belonged to the Maharajah of Bikaner—to 1898. In 1991, the Palace on Wheels was relaunched with all its former splendor, faithfully re-created down to the smallest detail, and gaining in efficient air-conditioning what it might have lost in authentic period charm. Its fourteen saloon cars are each named after one of the former princely states of Rajasthan, and the train also includes two dining cars, a bar and lounge car and four service cars.

Every Wednesday from September to April, the Palace on Wheels leaves the colorful tumult of Delhi Cantonment Railway Station to embark on a week-long luxury loop through Rajasthan, from the pink city of Jaipur to the blue city of Jodhpur, via the Thar Desert close to the border with Pakistan, before returning, via wildlife sanctuaries, deserted cities and romantic forts, to the lake city of Udaipur with its shimmering lake palaces. Pampered throughout, travelers might wonder what more wonders lie in store—and then, on the last day of the journey, comes the Taj Mahal, a magical end to a magical journey.

At one o'clock, the train. And I thought it was hot in the old days, reading *Kim* at Arcachon! ... The porters, who are insufferable, demand extra tips. Passepartout looks threatening, and they run away. They return to press their faces against the windows of the dining car, where all we can do is pass out—the precise words I think—to either side of a table.

I didn't know such heat was possible, that anyone could live in these infernal parts. The train moves off. ... And the searing flames of India lick at its metal, glass and wood until they blister with heat, drenching us in streams of stickiness, and coagulating in a sickening pall of heat, a cloying ooze churned by the paddles of the fans.

JEAN COCTEAU, 1936

280 Lounge car of the original Palace on Wheels, 1985.

289 Sawai Madho Singh II, the last ruling Maharajah of Jaipur, receiving the British Viceroy, who usually traveled in an immaculate white and gold train, in the 1890s. When the viceregal train visited Jaipur it did so on the Maharajah's private railway track, which led directly to his princely residence, the Rambagh Palace.

290 Indian passengers boarding a train at Madurai Station, photographed in verascope by Tartier, 1913. From the outset the Indian people took their railways to their hearts, creating a whole way of life around railway stations and railway travel. Night journeys in first and second class involved the provision of bedding rolls containing everything needed for a comfortable night's sleep: mattress, sheets, blankets, slippers and toilet articles. In other classes families also brought pots and pans to cook their meals.

291 The Palace on Wheels at Udaipur Station, 1985. Each carriage is named after one of the princely states of Rajasthan and bears the arms of the prince to whom the original carriage belonged. At every stop, passengers—like visiting dignitaries under the Raj—are received in the former royal palaces, now luxury hotels. In Jaipur they lunch at the Rambagh Palace (opened to the public in 1957); in Jodhpur at the Umaid Bhawan Palace (where the maharajah is still in residence);

285

We are still heading northwest, towards the Muslim land. My God, how beautiful this country is! Endless deserted plains, sometimes given a silvery sheen by rippling stands of tall white reeds. Stretching to the horizon, they raise their dry stems, tall and erect, topped by pale, trembling plumes, light as smoke. Occasionally a group of antelope will spring daintily away, before stopping stock still a moment, one hoof in the air, their graceful heads turned anxiously towards us. Storks and herons observe our passage with a solemn air. The great sky shimmers with light: in front of us the rails vanish into the distance, rigid, gleaming lines that meet far away, at a point that we shall never reach.

ANDRÉ CHEVILLON, 1891

286

and in Udaipur on the terrace of the Lake Palace Hotel.

292 I A Palace on Wheels locomotive, in the train's ivory livery festooned with flower garlands. Following the success of the Palace on Wheels, other luxury trains also now offer tours of Rajasthan. The Fairy Queen, which offers weekend tours from October to February to a select

complement of fifty passengers, boasts the world's oldest locomotive still in service. Built by the British firm Kitson, Thompson & Hewitson, it was built for the East India Railway Company in 1855.

293 I Palace on Wheels staff on duty in the lounge car. Some sixty employees attended each trip in the 1980s, with five soldiers providing security.

294 I One of the two Palace on Wheels dining cars, 1985. A week's trip on the Palace on Wheels is also considered as a gastronomic tour, with a choice of European and Indian cuisine. Rajasthani delicacies are a specialty.

295 I The Lake Palace Hotel on an island in Lake Pichola, Udaipur. It was in 1961 that the

Maharana of Udaipur decided to turn the enchanting white marble pleasure palace of Jag Niwas Palace, built in the mid-eighteenth century, into a hotel.

We continued our journey in the company of the Maharajah of Bharatpur. ... His private carriage was coupled to our own, and through the windows we could see his Rolls-Royces, trimmed in gold and silver, as they passed before him in procession before taking the road southwards. At the station at Mysore we were met by twelve maharajahs and as many rajahs. ... Our motorcars and those of the other princes were there, and as we set off on the road to the palace we formed an immense cortege.

VITOLD DE GOLISH, 1973

Our delegation comprised a mere thirty or so people, including Kamala [daughter of Raghubir Singh, Maharajah of Bundi], the Maharajah's second wife and his fifth, that is Jenny. As we were nearly two thousand kilometers from Mysore, Raghubir decided we should travel by train. Nonetheless, he ordered twenty of his most prestigious cars to go on ahead, in order to meet us from the train. . . .

Ramgopal arranged with the management of the railways that we should couple our three carriages to one of their trains. Raghubir's carriage was in precious wood lined with velvet: pink in the ladies' quarters and green in the gentlemen's. The gentlemen's accommodation was more spacious, consisting of a lounge with European-style armchairs, a sleeping cabin with a bathroom, and another compartment transformed into a shrine. This contained the statues of the family deities, Raghubir's ancestors, and a safe, sealed with impressive locks, holding the dynastic jewels and funds for the journey. The ladies' accommodation consisted of a large room arranged in the Indian manner, with rugs, cushions and mattresses for them to down on. Attached to it was a very comfortable bathroom.

VITOLD DE GOLISH, 1973

PALACE ON WHEELS

PALACE
ON
WHEELS

WDM 2B

16631

WDM 2B

16631

292

THE EASTERN AND ORIENTAL EXPRESS

1993

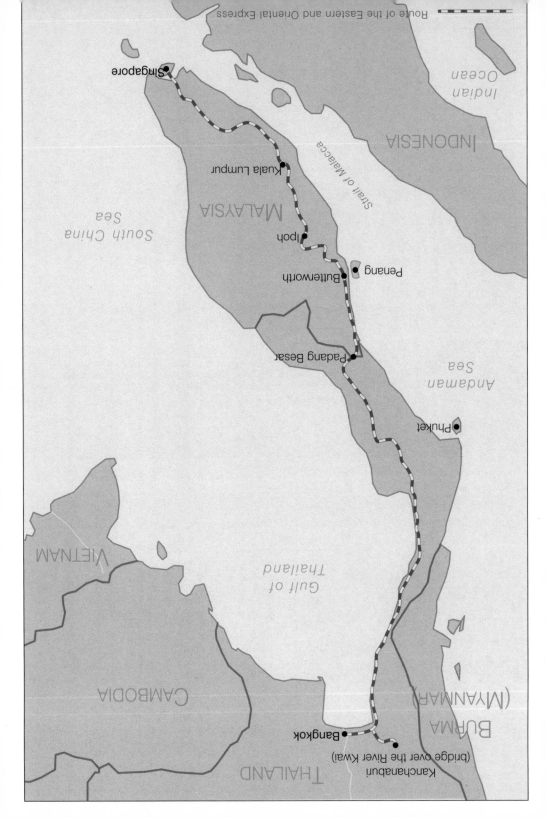

Route of the Eastern and Oriental Express

Indian
Ocean

INDONESIA

Singapore

Strait of Malacca

Kuala Lumpur

MALAYSIA

South China
Sea

Ipoh

Penang

Butterworth

Padang Besar

Andaman
Sea

Phuket

VIETNAM

Gulf of
Thailand

CAMBODIA

BURMA
(MYANMAR)

THAILAND

Bangkok

Kanchanaburi
(bridge over the River Kwai)

Virtually any backpacker who has ever succumbed to the charms of Southeast Asia will have fond memories of the Bangkok–Singapore railway line, some 1946 kilometers from north to south (or back again). The mildly adventurous, diverting and relatively thrifty version of this journey starts on board the International Express (Ekspress Antarabangsa in Malay, that departs Bangkok daily for Butterworth in Malaysia, pulling out of the grand Edwardian Hualamphong Station. Both trains, the Malaysian and the Thai, have their own special charm, and both are extremely comfortable, even in second class. It is fascinating—and a source of wonder—to watch the passenger coaches, with their rows of seats flanking a central aisle, metamorphosing with such apparent ease into long, pleasant dormitories, with cool, fresh sheets for each berth, a small bottle of water arranged on each pillow, and curtains to protect passengers' privacy. And then there are the showers, spacious metal compartments adorned only by a plughole in the middle of the floor. Clean, simple and accessible to all, the International Express is also a highly exotic experience for passengers inured to the discomforts of European railway travel (with the exception of luxury trains of course).

One of the joys of the Thai train is undoubtedly the unfailing courtesy of the staff—a requirement of the job, as

it turns out. Instructions posted in most Thai railway stations exhort employees to "Always smile, speak pleasantly and politely; be friendly, charming, helpful and courteous, try never to say no, keep calm to keep your job." Another is the dining car: lively, fun, busy and full of waiters balancing great dishes laden with chicken in coconut milk, shrimp soup or deep-fried pork. The food is good on the International Express. In Thailand, as in India, trains are the focus of a whole *art de vivre*, a beguiling cocktail of resourcefulness, ingenuity and authentic practical genius.

As you cross into Malaysia on the Langkawi Express from Hat Yai in Thailand to Kuala Lumpur, you leave this smiling culture behind you, as the staff keep courtesy to a minimum. It hardly matters though, as from Ipoh to Kuala Lumpur the vistas outside the windows are riveting in their splendor. The track winds through the red earth, between curtains of greenery so close that you could stretch out your hand and catch a liana as you pass. In the sultry heat, the palm fronds, tree ferns and lotus swamps of the jungle stretch to the foot of the blue mountains, beneath the white mists of the cloud forest. The overwhelming grandeur of this primeval jungle makes all the effort of getting here worthwhile.

For, delightful though the rail journey from Bangkok

Until 1916, when the southern part of the Royal State Railways of Siam was completed, the railway served only the Malay part of the peninsula, and travelers from Singapore to Bangkok had to go by sea. The west coast of the southern part of the peninsula, by contrast, was by this time well served. The peninsula's first railway line, a passenger and freight service opened in 1885 to export tin ore from Taiping to Port Weld (now Kuala Sepetang), was a great success, and within a few years railways were also serving the flourishing rubber industry. The architecture of the new railway stations reflects the optimism of this period of expansion, and the economic benefits it brought for the peninsula's British colonial rulers of the Straits Settlements. In 1910, the railway station at Kuala Lumpur was completed, a gleaming white mosque-like confection (by the British architect A.B. Hubback, who had served in India) of onion domes, minarets and lacy filigree in a neo-Moorish/Mughal style that was quickly dubbed "Anglo-marzipan." It is now served by local trains only, long-distance trains now stopping at the nearby Kuala Lumpur Central Station. On the island of Penang, the Malayan Railway Building of 1905, though less sumptuous, was possibly even more eccentric and certainly unique of its kind. This large and imposing structure boasted many notable features, including graceful arcades, a distinctive clock tower, extensive administrative offices, ticket offices, a waiting room and a stationmaster. It nevertheless lacked one attribute normally associated with railway stations: railway track. In fact the train stopped at Butterworth on the mainland, where in the 1920s British colonial officials would embark on the steamer to Hua Hin on the Gulf of Siam coast some 900 kilometers to the north, an exclusive resort where they would swim in their solar topees.

Although the railway crosses the border between Thailand and Malaysia, there had never been a direct service between Bangkok and Singapore until the inauguration of

to Singapore may be, it is not without its inconveniences. At Padang Besar, on the Thai-Malaysian border, all passengers have to disembark and wait—maybe for ten minutes, maybe for hours, according to the whim of the impassive border guards, who have been known to watch unperturbed as the connecting train pulls out, empty of passengers. Connections are another problem. At Butterworth and Kuala Lumpur all passengers have to change trains. When, as often happens, their train arrives too late to make the connection, they have no choice but to bed down and wait for the next departure.

the Eastern and Oriental Express in September 1993. The train is Japanese-built and from 1971 had run in New Zealand as the Silver Star, a luxury service between Auckland and Wellington, before being withdrawn in 1979. James Sherwood, the American millionaire who re-launched the vogue for luxury trains in the 1980s, bought its thirty-one carriages and had twenty of its passenger cars refurbished by the French designer Gérard Gallet (responsible for the Venice Simplon Orient Express) in Singapore. The finished train is an evocative hybrid of the Orient Express and Josef von Sternberg's fabulous *Shanghai Express* of 1932, combining colonial glamour with superb eastern craftsmanship, and featuring marquetry designs in fragrant woods and Malaysian motifs in Chinese and Thai lacquer and engraved mirrors.

Once a week, the Eastern and Oriental Express sets off, stopping twice en route for excursions to Penang island and the Bridge on the River Kwai. The rest of the three days and two nights of the journey is spent idling, taking tea in the lounge car, dinner in the piano bar, or a siesta in the cocooned privacy of one's own compartment with its bouquet of orchids. The service is impeccable, with—following the golden rule of luxury hotels—one

employee for every three passengers, and the unexpected bonus of an on-board palm-reader. Most wonderful of all is the observation car at the rear of the train, open to the sultry breezes and intoxicating perfumes of the jungle and the humming of insects. Whether you travel in luxury or relative simplicity, on the Bangkok–Singapore route it is the jungle, in the end, that will haunt your memories.

A few years ago, not far from Bukit-Gantang, a tigress and her cubs that were walking along the railway line arrived on the station platform. They stretched out to sleep beneath the ticket office window and the next day left; you could clearly see the imprint left in the dust by the folds of the tigress's skin as well as the broad traces of her paws and the smaller traces of the paws of her two cubs. ...Luckily, no passengers came to buy a ticket at the little station that night.

ROBERT FORAN, 1936

302

296 ı The Eastern and Oriental Express heading northwards up the Malay Peninsula, between Singapore and Butterworth.

305 ı Hualamphong Station, Bangkok's main railway station, from which trains head north and north-east, and—including the Eastern and Oriental Express—south. At eight o'clock sharp each morning the station comes to a standstill as the Thai national anthem is played over loudspeakers, and passengers and staff stand silently to attention.

306 ı In Hualamphong Station. Left: Destination boards waiting to be attached to carriages. Right: Before every departure this bell is rung to warn passengers to join their carriages.

307 ı The cathedral-like interior of Hualamphong Station, built in 1910–16 on the model of Manchester Central Station, which opened in 1880. The architecture of both stations focuses on the daring use of vast and unsupported single-span arches in cast iron. It was in the early 1920s that tracks were built heading westwards to the Burmese border and south to the Malay Peninsula.

308 ı Before heading south, the Eastern and Oriental Express makes a detour westwards to Kanchanaburi, a small town some 130 kilometers from Bangkok, near the infamous bridge on the River Kwai.

309 ı Poster and employee of the Eastern and Oriental Express. The logo and monogram of the E&O

The station [at Kuala Lumpur] must be the most beautiful in the world, and certainly its style and architecture are unique. The purpose of the building is not at first very clear, and one could be forgiven for taking it for a mosque. Furthermore, the snowy white of the two towers that rise at each end and like minarets gives it a Moorish appearance. Opposite is the Railway Administration building, built in the same style and, I am reliably informed, more decorative than functional. It appears that the costs incurred by the construction of these two buildings were excessive, when one remembers how long Pahang, Trengganu, Kelantan and the eastern parts of Johore had to wait for the railways they needed so badly.

ROBERT FORAN, 1936

make unambiguous reference to the world-renowned Eastern and Oriental Hotel in Penang: an elegant palace built overlooking the sea in the 1880s, which became the fashionable haunt of colonial administrators, rubber planters and an international elite including Rudyard Kipling, Noel Coward and Somerset Maugham. It was founded by the Sarkies brothers, proprietors of that other legend of Southeast Asian colonial hedonism, Raffles Hotel in Singapore.

310-311 ı Dining car on the Eastern and Oriental Express. In addition to the nostalgic reference to the Anglo-Malaysian palace of the same name, the Eastern and Oriental was also conceived as a tribute to the Orient Express. In the dining car, this close relationship is expressed in the glasses and silverware, exact copies of those of the legendary luxury train.

312-313 ı The Eastern and Oriental Express crossing the River Kwai Bridge. On the first excursion of the journey, passengers alight at River Kwai Station in order to visit the notorious bridge by boat. The bridge is one of the last vestiges of the Burma Railway, also known as the "Death Railway" built by the Japanese in 1942–43 in order to supply their troops in Burma. Working day and night, in sweltering heat and monsoon rains, some 61,000 prisoners of war (British, Dutch, Australian, American, Canadian and New

303

Between Butterworth and Singapore, c.1915.

Zealand) and 250,000 Asian forced laborers (mostly Thai; Malay and Burmese) built 415 kilometers (257 miles) of track in a mere 16 months (Japanese engineers had estimated five years for the job). But the cost was enormous: over 100,000 Asian laborers and 12–16,000 POWs are known to have perished, from disease (cholera, beri-beri, malaria, typhoid and dysentery), malnutrition, brutality, exhaustion or aerial bombardment. Crippled by Allied bombing 21 months after its completion, the railway was largely dismantled and abandoned after the war.

314 | Breakfast on board in the morning sun, amid exotic wood paneling and marquetry, orchids and inviting cushions. With over two thousand kilometers (1240 miles) of track and an average speed of 60kph (37mph), Eastern and Oriental Express passengers have ample time to savor life's little luxuries

315 | Left: Map of 1907 showing the railway network in the Straits Settlements and Federated Malay States.

316 | Thai workers in the rice paddies beside the Tha Chompu bridge.

317 | Landing stage for the Penang ferry, c.1910. Today's Eastern and Oriental Express arrives at Butterworth just after breakfast, allowing passengers a few hours to visit Penang, the first British colony on the Malay Peninsula, an uninhabited island ceded to the British East India Company by the Sultan of Kedah in 1786. Since 1985 a bridge has connected Penang to the mainland at Butterworth, but train passengers still take the ferry. Their visit to the island will naturally include dinner on the broad sea-front terrace of the Eastern and Oriental Hotel.

318 | Railway bridge at Kuala Lumpur, c.1915. On the far side of the bridge is the extravagant Anglo-Moorish building designed

by A.C. Norman in c.1896 to house the headquarters of the Federated Malay States Railway. On some services Kuala Lumpur is a compulsory and sometimes prolonged stop. Passengers who have to wait overnight for the next connection may choose to repair to the Heritage Station Hotel, housed in the spectacular colonial former station building.

319 | Verandah at the Raffles Hotel, Singapore, 1980s. Three days and two nights after leaving Bangkok, the Eastern and Oriental Express arrives in Singapore, a thriving international business centre that still retains a few reminders of colonial grandeur such as the inimitable Raffles Hotel, named after Singapore's founder, Sir Stamford Raffles and opened in 1887.

RIVER KWAI BRIDGE

สะพานข้ามแม่น้ำแคว

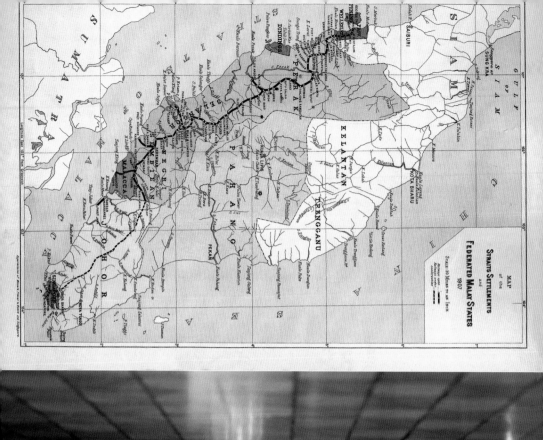

2000

RAILWAYS OF THE ANDES

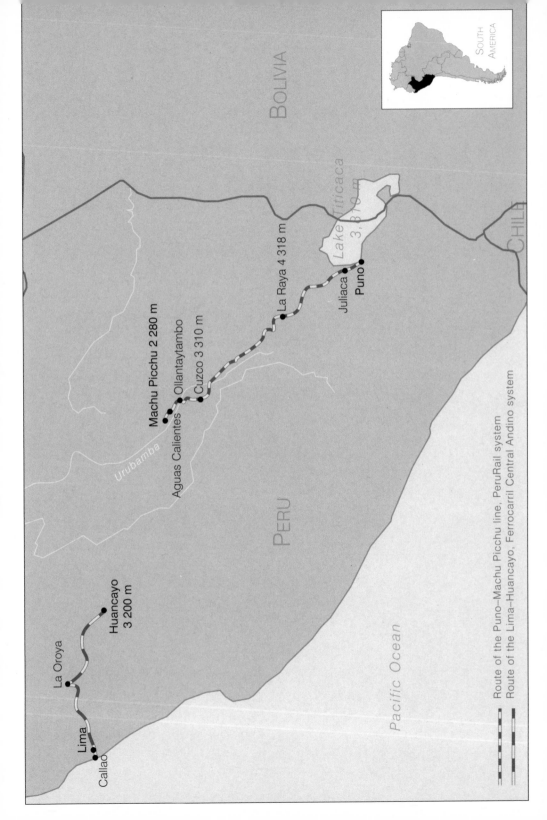

BOLIVIA

SOUTH AMERICA

PERU

CHILE

Lake Titicaca 3,810 m

La Raya 4 318 m

Machu Picchu 2 280 m

Ollantaytambo

Cuzco 3 310 m

Aguas Calientes

Juliaca

Puno

Urubamba

Huancayo 3 200 m

La Oroya

Lima

Callao

Pacific Ocean

Route of the Puno–Machu Picchu line, PeruRail system
Route of the Lima–Huancayo, Ferrocarril Central Andino system

Of the many adventurers cited as the possible inspiration for the figure of Indiana Jones, Hiram Bingham III is certainly a worthy contender. He possessed all the necessary requisites: a strict upbringing in an exotic location, as the son of New England Protestant missionaries to Honolulu; a degree from Yale in 1898, another from the University of California in 1900, and a doctorate from Harvard five years later; and a lectureship in South American history at Yale. Add to all this a flair for risky enterprises and a taste for the mysterious, and you have all the ingredients for the classic storybook adventurer.

All that remains to establish is the setting. In 1906 Bingham sailed to South America to follow the route that Bolívar had taken across Venezuela and Colombia in 1819. Two years later, after attending an academic conference in Chile, he took the steamer across Lake Titicaca to Peru. There he caught the train to Cusco, end of the line and hub of the Inca empire. Seduced by the colonial city, with its Spanish baroque churches built over the ruins of Inca temples to the sun, he returned to the Andes as leader of the Yale Peruvian Expedition, in search of lost cities of the Incas (as he would call his famous book). As on his first visit, he could reach no further than Cusco by train, so he made his own way to the

massive and mysterious pre-Inca fortress of Ollantaytambo. From here he set off by mule along the valley of the Urubamba River, covering some fifty kilometres before, on 24 July 1911, Bingham, with a surgeon, a botanist and Sergeant Carrasco of the Cusco police, was led by a peasant named Melchor Arteaga to site that was invisible from the valley. Among the lianas and tree roots, Bingham knew he had found something extraordinary. Archaeological expeditions sponsored by Yale and the National Geographic Society in 1912 and 1915 revealed that this was the ruins of the great Inca city of Machu Picchu, its temples, palaces and walls (with their astonishingly precise masonry) "lost" in the jungle for four centuries.

In 1913 work began on an extension of the railway line beyond Cusco, and in 1948 a rail link was finally established to Machu Picchu, bringing with it the tourists to whom the site had hitherto been inaccessible except by the same means as Bingham: on foot and mule back. The huge success of Bingham's book about his "discovery," *The Lost City of the Incas*, was to introduce the Inca city to the entire world—and vice versa, it seemed. Today it is one of the world's most popular tourist destinations, and since 2003 the name of Hiram Bingham has been adopted by a luxury train that conveys wealthy tourists from Cusco to Aguas Calientes (named after its thermal baths), the last village before the Inca city.

In its blue-and-gold livery, the Hiram Bingham leaves Poroy, a 20-minute coach ride from Cusco at nine o'clock in the morning daily except Sunday for a day-long tour. Breakfast is served while the train tackles the initial steep climb out of Cusco, before dropping down to the farmland of the Anta plateau, with its luxuriant gardens and colorful villages. At the altitude of Huarocondo the mountains close in as the track funnels into a gorge, and eventually the train reaches the Urubamba River, which flows through the Sacred Valley of the Incas. It is all too easy to imagine Bingham picking his way through this canyon on the back of a mule in the merciless sun. Then the train arrives at Ollantaytambo, where brunch is served in the two dining cars. Now it embarks on the last and most mysterious section of the journey, through tropical forest festooned with orchids, alive with hummingbirds, and punctuated by the ruins of Inca buildings and cultivation terraces.

The train's arrival at Aguas Calientes is carefully timed to coincide with other tour groups' departure from Machu Picchu for lunch, so it is in relative tranquility that the fortunate passengers of the Hiram Bingham are able to visit the ruins at their leisure, staying until sunset, with a short adjournment to the Sanctuary Lodge for afternoon tea. The return journey takes place amid the surrounding darkness and to the accompaniment of the chink of cocktail glasses, arriving in Poroy at nine-thirty at night, then coach to Cusco arriving at ten.

On Mondays, Wednesdays and Saturdays, those who wish can take the Andean Explorer, also run by PeruRail, in the opposite direction, from Cusco to Puno, with arrival at Lake Titicaca as its dramatic climax. This magnificent journey follows the Huatanay River through green pampas dotted with willow and eucalyptus and grazed by vicuna, before joining the Vilcanota River as it plunges in to its gorge. At last you catch your first glimpse of the vast marshlands and reed beds of Puno Bay, with Lake Titicaca, the world's highest navigable lake, beyond.

But do not believe anyone who tells you that this line is the world's highest, culminating in the pass of La Raya at 4318m (just over 14,000ft), where the train makes a dramatic pause. Until 2006 (when China's railway to Lhasa in Tibet opened) that distinction went to the line from Lima to Huancayo, known as the Central Railway, which peaks in the tunnel of La Galera, at 4786m (nearly 16,000ft). The fact that no connection exists between these two railways reflects the difficult and piecemeal history of the Peruvian railways and the challenging topography of Peru. War with Chile in 1879–83 halted work and destroyed large sections of track; and complex financial negotiations involving Peruvian guano and British bonds resulted in little actual building work.

As early as 1851, nonetheless, plans were in hand to extend the Lima–Callao railway, opened that year. By 1868 the route had been finalized, and a swashbuckling American entrepreneur by the name of Henry "Honest Harry" Meiggs, otherwise known as the Yankee Pizarro, had been summoned to take charge of the work. Meiggs had already made his name by building a railway in Chile within his budget and ahead of schedule. The railway he now set out to build, consisted of one apparently insuperable technical challenge after another, at an altitude where no such venture had ever been attempted before. Boasting "I will lay tracks where llamas walk," Meiggs succeeded in building the world's highest railway and its highest railway bridge at that time, and the longest succession of zigzags on any railway. He has a fitting memorial in Mount Meiggs, a peak visible from the end of Galera tunnel.

Meanwhile the vicissitudes of the Peruvian railway system continued into the twentieth century: in the 1930s many lines were replaced by other modes of transport, and in more recent years much of the network around Lima was shut down. In the twenty-first century the potential benefits to the tourist industry have become more obvious, and Peru's railways have been largely refurbished. Now a newly equipped train leaves Lima's Desamparados Station approximately twice a month for Huancayo. On its vertiginous journey it passes through 68 tunnels, negotiates 9 switchbacks and crosses 61 bridges, including the celebrated Verrugas viaduct which spans a gorge 175m wide and 80m deep. Breathtaking is the only word for it, not only metaphorically but also literally. Passengers can be reassured, however: the train is permanently staffed by a first aider equipped with oxygen supplies.

320 I The Andean Explorer, operated by PeruRail, halted at the La Raya pass on the Cusco–Puno line.

329 I A PeruRail service leaving Ollantaytambo en route for Machu Picchu. The lines from Cusco to Machu Picchu and Puno are now both operated by PeruRail, a subsidiary of the British-owned Orient-Express company. In addition to the deluxe Hiram Bingham, PeruRail also offers two more affordable alternatives for tourists on this route: the panoramic Vistadome, and the more basic Backpacker. In accordance with an agreement with the Peruvian government, PeruRail also offers local train services (out of bounds to tourists) at very low prices for inhabitants of the region, operating at a loss.

330-331 I Trains on the Central Railway from Lima to Huancayo, 1985. On these railways of the high Andes, where some stations lie at over 4000m, changing from steam to diesel haulage was no simple matter. The first diesel locomotives on this line, of American manufacture, required technical modification to make them suitable for operation at high altitudes. With steam engines there was never a problem: as water boils at 60 degrees Celsius at that altitude, the higher they climbed the more efficient they became.

332-333 I The Cusco–Puno line in the region of Lake Titicaca, 1985.

334-335 I The Cusco–Puno train crossing the altiplano at the altitude of the La Raya pass, 1985. On the high pampas, large herds of llama, alpaca, vicuna and guanaco roam free.

336-337 I The Andean Explorer between Cusco and Puno. The first-class accommodation in this train is laid out in the style of Pullman coaches from the 1920s.

338 I Rounding a bend near El Arco, after the climb out of Cusco.

339 I View over Cusco as the train climbs through the city outskirts on its way to Machu Picchu.

340 I A Vistadome train in the station at Ollantaytambo, 2004. This photo was taken from the El Albergue hotel, a small stylish bed-and-breakfast establishment

The station at Juliaca,
between Puno and
Cusco, in the 1920s.

housed in a former station annex, with its front door opening straight on to the platform. Ollantaytambo's oldest hostel, El Albergue has been run by an American couple, and artist and a writer, since 1976.

341 | A PeruRail employee coupling two Vistadome trains together in the station at Ollantaytambo, 2004. Apart from going on foot, the train is the only way to reach Machu Picchu. Tourists can go as far as Ollantaytambo by coach, but then have to transfer to the railway.

342 | Peruvian children have fun jumping on and off the running boards of a slow-moving train, 1985.

343 | Early morning in the station at Ollantaytambo, 2004. There is a bustle of activity as everyone prepares for the arrival of the day's tourists: porters offering their service to those planning to hike the Inca Trail, and souvenir sellers taking their wares to Aguas Calientes.

344 | Musicians playing on board a PeruRail luxury service.

345 | As a Vistadome train north-east of Chillca heads towards Machu Picchu, passengers can observe the progress of the progress of walkers on the Inca Trail, on the opposite bank of the Urubamba River. This 43km track, hewn out of the rock by the Incas, leads directly to Machu Picchu and is the most popular trek in Peru.

346 | In the Urubamba valley near Machu Picchu.

347 | The open observation car on a PeruRail luxury service.

348 | Arrival at Aguas Calientes, a small village below Machu Picchu. From here tourists catch a bus up to the Inca city.

349 | A scheduled service for local people, 1990s.

350 | The Hiram Bingham emerging from a tunnel built in 1928, en route for Machu Picchu.

351 | Passing through Aguas Calientes, 1985. Accessible only by train, the village lives around the arrival and departure of trains, and of the tourists they bring.

352 | A station lost in the pampas, somewhere on the Puno–Cusco line.

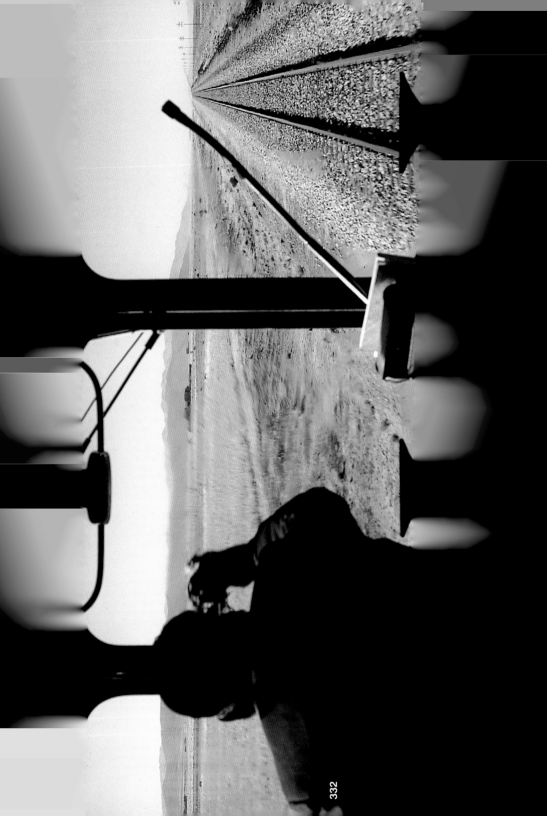

334

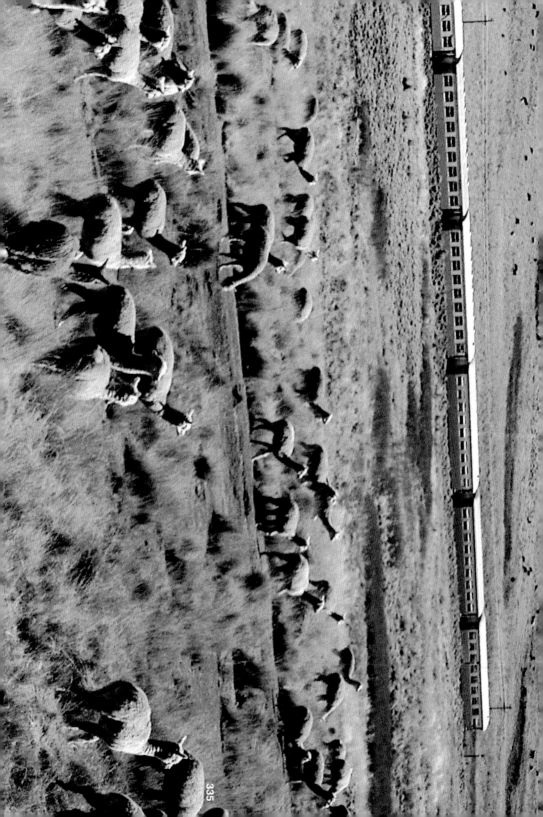

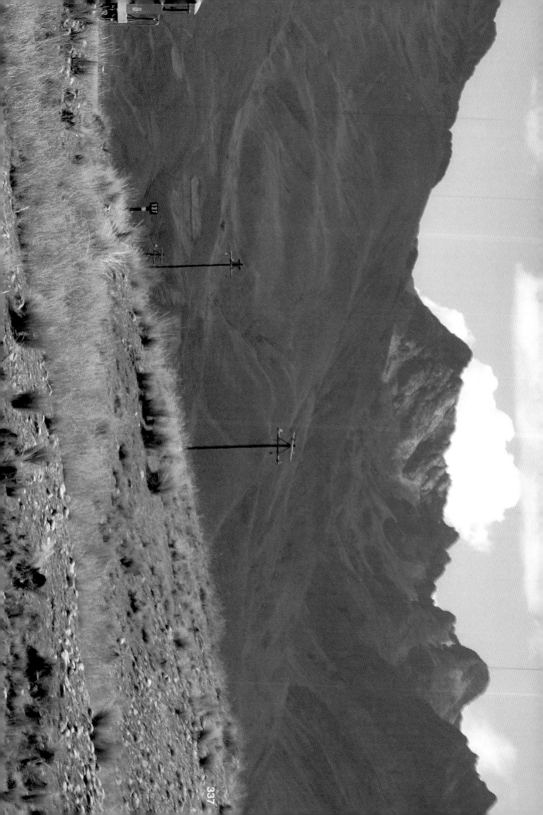

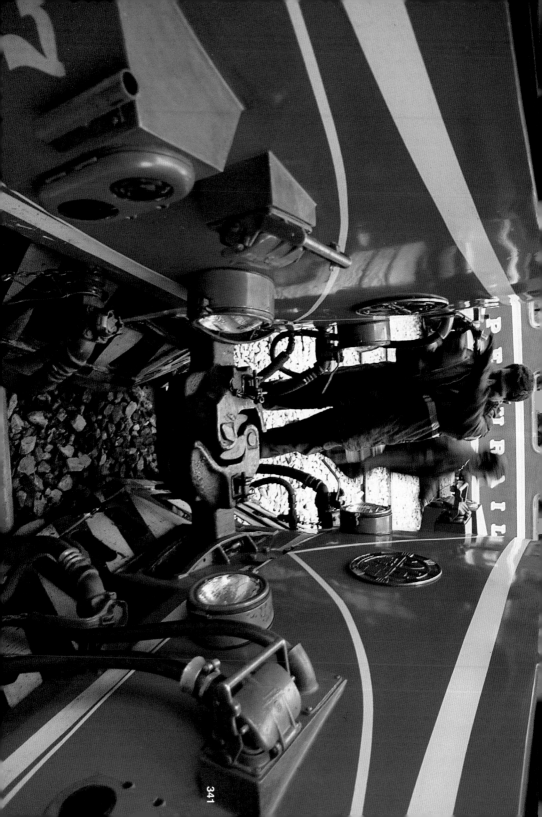

Index of proper names

Citations

Page 31
Émile Delmas, *Java, Ceyla « Les Indes », excursion sous l'équateur et la zone torride*, Paris, Librairie de l'art, 1898

Page 32
Hugues Krafft, *Souvenirs de notre tour du monde*, Paris, Librairie Hachette et Cie, 1885

Pages 33, 34
André Chevillon, *Dans l'Inde*, Paris, Librairie Hachette et Cie, 1891

Page 36
Claudine Canetti, *L'Inde buissonnière*, ed. Albin Michel, Paris, 1961

Pages 60, 62, 64
Edmond About, *De Pontoise à Stamboul*, Hachette, 1883

Page 61
Georges Boyer, *Le Figaro*, 20 octobre 1883

Page 63
Paul Morand, *Venises*, L'imaginaire/Gallimard, 1983

Page 94
Philippe Deschamps, *Vingt mille lieux à travers le monde dédié à la jeunesse studieuse de France et de Russie, récits des voyages faits par P. Deschamps en Europe, Asie, Afrique et Amérique*, E. Leroux éditeur, Paris, 1900

Page 95
Jack London, *The Road*, 1907

Page 132
Albert Roussy, *De Genève à Irkoutsk*, 1883 (www.cottier.org/siteatelier/siberie/txtirkou.html)

Page 133
John Forster Fraser, *The Real Siberia*, Cassel and Co, Londres 1902

Page 134
Théophile Gautier, *Voyage en Russie*, Charpentier, Paris, 1866

Page 136
M. G. Weulersse, *Au Petchili et sur les frontières de Mandchourie*, 1901

Page 166, 167
Charles Miller, *The Lunatic Express: An Entertainment in Imperialism*, MacDonald & Co., London, 1972

Page 198
Lucien Solvay, *Au pays des orangers*, 1882

Page 199
F. Scott Fitzgerald, *Tender is the Night*, Scribner, New York, 1995

Pages 200, 204
Agatha Christie, *Le train bleu*, Librairie des Champs-Élysées, Paris, 1947

Page 203
Colette, *Prisons et Paradis*, Ferenczi et fils, Paris, 1932

Pages 226, 227, 228
Ethel. M. Bagg, *Voyage dans l'Afrique du Sud*, revue Le Tour du Monde, Hachette, 1913

Pages 250, 252
Hugues Krafft, *Souvenirs de notre tour du monde*, Paris, Librairie Hachette et Cie, 1885

Pages 251, 255, 256
Isabella L. Bird, *Voyage d'une femme aux montagnes Rocheuses*, Librairie Plon, 1888

Page 285
Jean Cocteau, *Tour du Monde en 80 jours (mon premier voyage)*, Idées/Gallimard, Paris, 1983

Page 286
André Chevillon, *Dans l'Inde*, Paris, Librairie Hachette et Cie, 1891

Pages 287, 288
Vitold de Golish, *L'Inde impudique des maharajahs*, Laffont, Paris, 1973

Pages 302, 303
W. Robert Foran, *La vie en Malaisie, Singapour-Malacca-Bangkok-Sumatra-Java-Bali*, Payot, Paris, 1936

Bibliography

100 trains de légende, André Papazian, Solar, 2003

All Aboard !, Images from the Golden Age of Rail Travel, Lynn Johnson & Michael O'Leary, Chronicle Books, San Francisco

Des trains pas comme les autres, François Gall, Bernard d'Abrigeon, Sélection du Reader's Digest, 2002

Histoire des trains de luxe, George Behrend, Medea, 1984

India's world Heritage Line, Richard Wallace, published by the friends of DHR, 2000

L'Orient-Express, Jean des Cars, Jean-Paul Caracalla, Denoël, 1984

Le goût du voyage, Jean-Paul Caracalla, Compagnie des Wagons-Lits/ Flammarion, 2001

Le Train Bleu, Jean des Cars, Jean-Paul Caracalla, Denoël, 1988

Le Transsibérien, Jean des Cars, Jean-Paul Caracalla, Denoël, 1986

Les derniers trains de rêve, Patrick Poivre d'Arvor, Le Chêne /Filipacchi, 1991

Les grands trains, Clive Lamming, Larousse, 2001

Les plus beaux voyages en train, ouvrage collectif, Solar, 1994

Union Pacific Railroad, Brian Solomon, MBI Publishing Company, 2000

Photographic credits

Alamy Images: pp. 150, 151, 292, 293

Bailey, Krys/Marmotta: p. 352

Brown, Steve: pp. 88, 102, 104, 106, 107, 108, 109, 110–111, 137, 145, 146, 155–158, 274–275

Brzostowski, Rob E.: pp. 340, 341, 343, 345

Burlington Northern Santa Fe: p. 262

Calzephyr.railfan.net: pp. 263, 264 (right), 277

Charlesworth, David: pp. 37, 38, 39, 40–41, 42, 43, 51

Compagnie des Wagons-Lits: pp. 2, 4, 11, 17, 57, 58, 64, 65 (vignette), 66, 67, 68, 69, 70, 71, 72, 75, 76, 79, 84, 85, 139, 140, 141, 152, 153, 201, 202, 203, 205, 207, 208, 209, 210, 211, 212, 213, 214, 215, 216, 218

Darjeeling Himalayan Railway: pp. 29, 35, 44

Diaporama: pp. 309 (right), 313, 351

Donzel, Catherine: pp. 121, 123

Eastern & Oriental Express: pp. 296, 308, 309 (left), 310, 311, 312, 314, 315, 316

Gert, Ludwig/Visum/Cosmos: p. 124

Gysemberg, Benoît: pp. 6–7, 112, 113, 159, 160, 174, 175, 176–177, 178, 179, 184–185, 244, 264 (left), 265, 266, 267, 278, 280, 291, 330, 331, 342, 332, 333, 334–335, 294

Laubier, Guillaume de: p. 78

Martin, Terry: pp. 46, 47

McBeath, Malcolm: p. 344

Navez, Ren: p. 249

Orient-Express Limited: pp. 320, 336–337, 346, 347, 348, 350

Roger-Viollet: pp. 52, 192, 217, 257, 276

Seiler, Bernd: p. 24

Sharma, Anil: p. 295

The Blue Train: pp. 220, 229, 231–243

Tindall, Nick: p. 338

Tipple, Marion: p. 329

Vérascopes-Richard/Photothèque Hachette: pp. 49 (Lafarelle), 142 (Turot), 143 (Turot), 144 (Chemin-Duponté), 147 (Kritch), 148–149, 154 (Zo d'Axa), 169 (Voyage Alluaud), 170 (Voyage Alluaud), 180 (Alluaud), 183 (Alluaud), 186 (Alluaud), 190 (Alluaud), 230 (Chemin-Duponté), 279 (Wallon)

Via Rail: pp. 103, 115, 116–117, 118, 182, 188, 305, 306, 307

Waite, James: pp. 171, 173, 181,

Walter, Marc: pp. 8, 12, 19, 45, 48, 50, 65, 74, 77, 80, 81, 82, 83, 86, 87, 101, 114, 119, 120, 122, 138, 206, 219, 258, 259, 260, 261, 289, 290, 304, 317, 318, 319, 327

Waring, Claire/Buzzwords Editorial: p. 339

Warren, Geoff: pp. 1, 18, 172, 187, 189, 191

Acknowledgments

The editorial team wishes to thank the photographers and all the train buffs who have contributed to this work. Their information has been invaluable to us. We also wish to thank the railway companies—The Blue Train, Orient-Express Ltd, Via Rail, Eastern and Oriental Express—which have furnished us with important documentation. Our recognition goes particularly to the Compagnie des Wagons-Lits, represented by Mrs. Martine Chantereau, which has enormously contributed to the enrichment of this book. Thanks to the documents they entrusted to us and which we have reproduced here, we hope to contribute to a better understanding of the brilliant heritage of the Compagnie, a heritage preserved and extended thanks to Pullman Orient Express which carries on the adventure begun now more than a century ago.

First published in the United States of America by
The Vendome Press, 1334 York Avenue, New York, N.Y. 10021

© Éditions du Chêne-Hachette-Livre 2006
Translation copyright © 2007 The Vendome Press

All rights reserved. No part of the contents of this book may be reproduced without written permission of the publisher.

ISBN 13: 978-0-86565-188-3

Library of Congress Cataloging-in-Publication Data
Poivre d'Arvor, Patrick.
[Âge d'or du voyage en train. English]
First class : legandary train journeys around the world / Patrick Poivre d'Arvor.
p. cm.
Includes index.
ISBN 978-0-86565-188-3 (hardcover & slipcase : alk. paper)
1. Railroad travel. I. Title.
G151.P6313 2007
910.4--dc22
2007026874

10 9 8 7 6 5 4 3 2 1

Printed in China by Midas